THE WELLESLEY
COOKIE
EXCHANGE
COOKBOOK

SUSAN MAHNKE PEERY

A FIRESIDE BOOK
PUBLISHED BY SIMON & SCHUSTER INC.
NEW YORK LONDON TORONTO SYDNEY TOKYO SINGAPORE

Designed by Kay Lee

Illustrations by Lisa Amoroso

Manufactured in the United States of America

10 9 8 7 6 5   Pbk.

Library of Congress Cataloging in Publication Data

Peery, Susan Mahnke.
  The Wellesley cookie exchange cookbook.

  "A Fireside Book"
  Includes index.
  1. Cookies. I. Title.
[TX772.P36   1988]   641.8′654   88-4450

ISBN 0-671-66588-X   Pbk.

CONTENTS

ACKNOWLEDGMENTS

I have been baking cookies with great enthusiasm since an early age, and for this happy circumstance I thank my mother, Margaret Mahnke, who taught me how. (I, in turn, look forward to teaching my daughter, Molly.) Mary Bevilacqua, Laurel Gabel, and all of the members of the Wellesley Cookie Exchange provided both the inspiration and the substance of this book. We met in 1982 when I wrote an article about the cookie exchange for the Great New England Cooks series in Yankee magazine. Some of the recipes have been drawn from a cookbook that Mary and Laurel published in 1980; the recipes are reprinted here with permission. A Collection of Holiday Favorites, containing recipes and menus for year-round use, can be obtained by writing to Mary Bevilacqua at 10 Wall Street, Wellesley, MA 02181, or to Laurel Gabel at 215 Fishers Road, Pittsford, NY 14534.

Once this project got under way, many friends contributed moral support, cookie tasting, and even their favorite recipes. This is in the true spirit of the cookie exchange, and I am grateful. I especially thank Gordon Peery and Sandy Taylor.

S.M.P.

INTRODUCTION
The Great Annual Wellesley Christmas Cookie Exchange

One snowy evening just before Christmas in 1971, friends, neighbors, and relatives of Mary Bevilacqua and Laurel Gabel walked up the curving path to Mary's home on a quiet side street in Wellesley, Massachusetts, to gather for their first Christmas cookie exchange. Every year since, the event has been repeated until it has become as much a part of their annual Christmas ritual as trimming the tree. Many of the women see each other only once a year, at the cookie exchange, but feel a warm camaraderie through this traditional gathering.

The cookie exchange is a wonderful occasion for dressing up, eating loads of tempting holiday food, sipping wassail and heady eggnog, and having a fine time socializing with friends whose busy lives intersect all too seldom. But at eight o'clock, Mary and Laurel ring a little silver bell and all of the guests turn to the serious business at hand: exchanging cookies. Each participant has brought a batch of cookies—perhaps a family favorite like thumbprint cookies, or an heirloom recipe such as *Zimtsterne* or almond *crostata*, or extra-fancy holiday cookies like frosted sugar plums or perky gingerbread men. One by one, the trays of cookies are passed around as each baker describes the origin of the cookie and any idiosyncracies of the recipe. Each woman selects one or two cookies from each batch until she has assembled a collection of several dozen different cookies, delicious booty to serve family and guests during the busy holiday season at hand.

There are cookies whose recipes emigrated across the Atlantic generations ago from Italy, Germany, Austria, Norway; cookies rich with sweet butter and nutmeats and with frosting as lavish as velvet and old lace; cookies baked by busy hands and redolent not only of spices and citrus but also of tradition, fellowship, and the love of giving. That's what each person brings and takes home every year from the cookie exchange.

Recipe swopping is also an important part of the cookie exchange, a chance to collect rules and tips from other expert bakers. Over the years the Wellesley ladies have amassed an extensive collection of cookie recipes, which start on page 15. They also offer suggestions for putting on a successful cookie exchange as well as all the basic information anyone needs to know in order to bake, decorate, and store cookies at Christmas or any time during the year (see Chapter 1: A Cookie Primer).

HOW TO START YOUR OWN COOKIE EXCHANGE

All you need are a few cookie-loving friends and a place to gather. You can model your cookie exchange on the Wellesley group's, or devise your own method. Remember, if you do it twice, at least *someone* will think it's a tradition!

Well in advance of Christmas, set a date for the cookie exchange (Mary and Laurel usually hold theirs on a weeknight about two weeks before Christmas), and send invitations to as many people as you can comfortably accommodate. (Mary and Laurel have had as many as thirty people happily crowded into Mary's living room—along with thirty batches of cookies!) Tell each person you invite to bring at least three dozen special cookies of one kind, and to bring along an empty container that will hold the just desserts of the cookie exchange. (Hard-core cookie collectors bring lots of little plastic bags to separate cookie varieties so that the flavors won't mingle, and tuck crumpled waxed paper into the interstices of the box so that delicate cookies won't be crushed.) If you object to cigarettes, you might tactfully request, as Mary and Laurel do on their invitation, that smokers refrain from lighting up at the cookie exchange.

Mary and Laurel invite their friends to come at about 7:30 P.M., and plan to serve a candlelight buffet of Christmas desserts and beverages (for recipes, see suggestions starting on page 217). These luscious treats—Yule log (a cream-filled chocolate cake roll), almond puff, English trifle, cider wassail, cranberry punch, peach brandy eggnog— not only make an elegant and festive Christmas buffet, but also numb everyone's sweet tooth so that the prized cookies will survive unscathed and unnibbled (for the most part). Mary and Laurel also bake an extra batch of cookies for emergency use by someone who wants to come but is unable, for one reason or another, to bake cookies.

At the Wellesley Cookie Exchange, Mary's house is beautifully decorated for Christmas, luminaria line the walk, and nearly everyone gets dressed up. Mary and Laurel traditionally wear long skirts and lacy white aprons. It all helps make the event seem special. But a cookie exchange can support any degree of formality or informality, as long as the cookies are good, so don't wear yourself out being fancy if that's not your style—the point is to have a good time.

As people arrive on the appointed evening, Mary and Laurel store the boxes of cookies in an out-of-the-way place while everyone enjoys the buffet, then gently herd guests into the living room, bring in all the cookies and display them on a large coffee table, and start the exchange. One tray of cookies at a time is handed carefully around the room as its baker describes the contents, where she got the recipe, and any pitfalls she might have encountered. Cookie-baking tips and humorous anecdotes fly fast and furious among these friends. Some of the participants make a point of making a different cookie each year; others rely on a tried-and-true favorite. Mary's neighbor, Eleanor Homeyer, has been coming to the cookie exchange since the first year. "I've always made gingerbread boys," she said, "except for one year when I thought I'd try something different. But you should have seen how everyone's face fell when I didn't bring the gingerbread boys! So I'm back to making them. I've used the same recipe since the 1920s, when I made them with my own mother, always on the first day of Christmas vacation."

At the end of the evening, after the guests have departed, Mary and Laurel take out their cookie exchange notebook to record that year's guest list, what was served at the buffet, and what kinds of cookies were swopped. It's a useful little archive and also a source of many pleasant recollections.

1. A COOKIE PRIMER:

Expert Advice on Ingredients, Equipment, Preparation, and Storage

INGREDIENTS

Butter, sugar, an egg, perhaps some chocolate or nuts, enough flour to bind the dough—that's what cookies are made of, basically, and the hundreds of kinds of cookies that we bake are just variations on this theme. As in all other areas of cooking, using fresh, high-quality ingredients is critical to success. Butter, nuts, chocolate, coconut, spices, and other components are expensive, but worthwhile. Watch for sales and coupon discounts in grocery stores and buy ahead: butter and nuts keep well in the freezer; chocolate and many other ingredients can be stored in a cool spot in the cupboard. Many bakers start stockpiling Christmas baking ingredients in September to lessen the shock on the weekly grocery budget.

Shortening: For flavor, there is no substitute for *butter*. Cookies made with butter have outstanding taste and a finely grained, often crisp texture. Butter also helps cookies to keep well and maintain their flavor. Many seasoned cookie bakers use only butter in baking, and some go a step further and use unsalted butter (called sweet butter) for extra lightness. Salt can toughen dough, although the amount of salt in salted butter is probably not enough to make a big difference. If your pocketbook and cholesterol count permit, it's best to use butter, especially in pressed cookies, plain butter cookies, or any delicate cookie in which the flavor of the shortening will be pronounced.

Margarine, which may be substituted in equal amounts for butter, tends to create a chewy cookie, and where that is desirable, it's an excellent choice.

Solid vegetable shortening, also a measure-for-measure substitute, can yield good results in soft, moist cookies, and will help retain a nice rounded shape in drop cookies. Liquid *vegetable oil* is occasionally used in cookie baking, but cannot be substituted for solid shortening without disastrous results.

The new *butter/margarine* combinations can be used

with acceptable results in almost any recipe in this book. Always use solid butter or margarine and not the whipped variety.

Shortenings should be brought to room temperature, unless otherwise noted. If you are counting calories, there is virtually no difference between any of these fats.

Flour: We recommend using an all-purpose unbleached flour for the recipes in this book, unless a recipe specifies otherwise. Substituting whole-grain flour for part or all of the all-purpose flour in a recipe will make the cookie heavier and grainier; granulated flour (such as Wondra) produces sandy-textured drop cookies; self-rising flour, unless used with a recipe specifically formulated for it, will leave you in the dark about how much salt and leavening to use, since it already contains predetermined amounts of those substances.

Excessive flour in a recipe can create hard, dry cookies. When mixing cookies, don't add all the flour at once: the amount of humidity in the air will affect the amount of moisture that the flour can absorb, and will thus affect the quantity of flour to use. It's better to add just enough to keep the cookie dough from being too sticky than to add too much (in which case you need to readjust other ingredients, and you're probably in a bit of trouble). It is usually unnecessary to sift flour before measuring: simply spoon or scoop it lightly into a measuring cup without packing it, and use a knife to level off the measure.

Eggs: Use only fresh eggs, of course, and at room temperature. Most recipes assume that you will be using large eggs, which have a volume of about ¼ cup each.

Sweeteners: *Granulated sugar* is used most frequently in cookie making: when a recipe calls simply for "sugar," it is safe to assume that granulated sugar is intended. *Powdered* or *confectioners' sugar*, also called 10X, contains a small amount of cornstarch, and is used in some finely textured cookies. *Brown sugar*, which contains molasses, tends to produce chewy, dark cookies with a caramel flavor. Both light and dark brown sugar should be packed firmly into a cup for measuring. To store brown sugar, add a wedge of apple to keep it from hardening. *Liquid sugars*, such as maple syrup, honey, molasses, and corn syrup, are used primarily for their flavors.

Sugars tenderize as well as sweeten. Substituting one kind of sugar for another will alter the character of a cookie. Swopping dry and liquid sugars calls for drastic adjustments in other ingredients, and is not recommended.

Chocolate: Recipes may specify bitter (also called unsweetened or baking) chocolate, semi-sweet (such as the chocolate chips commonly used in Toll House cookies), or sweet. Cocoa (the unsweetened powder, not a mix) is also called for in some recipes. Be sure to use the type of chocolate specified, as substitutions may not be successful. For dipping pretzels, you can buy what is called "dipping chocolate" at party-goods stores: this usually contains paraffin and other ingredients to make the chocolate more silky when melted. Imitation chocolate has an undesirable flavor. White "chocolate" contains no chocolate at all, but is a mixture of vegetable fats, coloring, and flavors.

The safest way to melt chocolate is in a double boiler over hot water, or in a microwave oven. Experienced cooks sometimes place chocolate in a heavy saucepan over direct low heat, but that method carries the risk of scorching.

Most recipes that call for chocolate also require vanilla. The flavors are extremely compatible, and vanilla seems to enhance the essence of chocolate.

Nuts: Unless they are still in sealed cans or cellophane bags, nuts can become rancid quickly (in just a week or two, depending on conditions) at room temperature, and should be stored in the refrigerator or freezer. Follow the example of our furry friends and squirrel away bags of walnuts, pecans, and almonds before the Christmas baking season—it's like money in the bank! When a recipe calls for chopped nuts, it usually means walnuts or pecans. Almonds, with their delicate flavor, and peanuts, which are more assertive, should be used only when specified.

Leavening: *Baking powder* (always the double-acting kind, which nine times out of ten is the only kind your grocery store carries anyway) and *baking soda* are not interchangeable. Nevertheless, if you run out of baking powder, you may substitute ½ teaspoon of baking soda plus ½ teaspoon cream of tartar for every teaspoon of baking powder required. (There is no precise substitute for baking soda.) Whipped *egg whites* and *yeast* are two other forms of leavening used in recipes in this book.

Spices and Extracts: Because these flavorings make such a critical flavor difference in cookies, we recommend using only the finest and freshest spices and extracts you can find. Use them discriminatingly but courageously. A touch of almond extract in a plain sugar-cookie recipe (add about ½ teaspoon at the same time you add the eggs to the dough), or a good dash of cardamom in spicy applesauce bars (add ½ teaspoon cardamom along with the other spices) makes a subtle but significant difference. We recommend using only pure vanilla extract, never imitation, even though you can buy quarts of the imitation stuff for the price of one good bottle of pure vanilla. The taste of imitation vanilla is immediately detected, and is exaggerated if the dough or cookies are frozen.

Other Ingredients: When you see *oatmeal* in a list of ingredients, it means uncooked rolled oats, either old-fashioned or quick, but not instant.

Coconut means the shredded or flaked and sweetened kind. If you have fresh coconut, grate it and soak it in milk, refrigerated, for about 6 hours, then drain. This will give it about the same moisture content as the packaged kind.

Raisins, which may be used interchangeably with

chopped dates in most recipes, are the dark Thompson seedless variety, unless golden raisins are specified. *Currants* and *muscat raisins* are occasionally used. Raisins should be plump and soft. If they seem dry and hard, soak them in hot water for 15 or 20 minutes, then drain before using.

Grated *orange* and *lemon rind* (known as "zest" these days) refers to the outer colored portion of the rind.

Always use solid *cream cheese* and not the whipped variety.

EQUIPMENT

You can make perfectly wonderful cookies with a minimum of equipment: measuring cup and spoons, mixing bowl, wooden spoon, cookie sheet, and cooling rack. But dedicated cookie makers tend to accumulate a few more things, such as:

• Heavy-duty mixers for stirring large batches of cookie dough. (Hand-held portable mixers are usually not powerful enough to mix stiff cookie dough.) Food processors may be useful for creaming butter and sugar, but unless the processor bowl is quite large, this necessitates transferring the mixture to a mixing bowl to finish the job. We're willing to bet that 95 percent of cookie bakers use a large ceramic or stainless-steel mixing bowl, a wooden spoon, and lots of elbow grease.

• Three heavy-duty cookie sheets, in a size that will allow 2 inches clearance all around on the oven rack. Many cookbooks advise against using cookie sheets with rims, on the theory that the rims interfere with air circulation, but we have used rimmed cookie sheets and jelly-roll pans (15" x 10" x 1") for years with no problems. If you have three cookie sheets, one can be in the oven and one can be cooling off while the third is being filled with cookie dough. Be sure the sheets are flat and not warped.

Fairly new on the market are insulated cookie sheets, which help keep cookie bottoms from burning.

♦ A pastry cloth for rolling out gingerbread boys and other cut-out cookies. It reduces problems with sticky dough. You may want to tack the pastry cloth to a large breadboard. Flour it lightly before starting to roll the dough.

♦ An intriguing assortment of cookie cutters. Because we make cut-out cookies year-round, not only at Christmas, we have lips and hearts (Valentine's Day), chicks and bunnies (Easter), musical notes (for our favorite musician's birthday), butterflies and ducklings (fun for summer parties), and a dog bone (for our loyal canine's birthday). You can also buy sets of interlocking cookie cutters that allow you to cut out an entire area of rolled dough without any waste. Very efficient!

♦ A rolling pin that feels comfortable to you. (Hollow rolling pins that can be filled with ice help keep the dough cool while you roll, as long as the ice water doesn't leak out.)

♦ A long-bladed metal spatula for taking delicate cookies off cookie sheets.

♦ A cookie press with assorted disks for making spritz.

♦ A pastry bag for decorating.

♦ Several cooling racks (useful in bread baking, candy making, and other kitchen endeavors).

PREPARATION

Ingredients and Equipment: Have all ingredients at room temperature before starting to mix the cookie dough. Good cooks always grease cookie sheets unless the recipe specifically says not to do this. Apply a light coating of vegetable shortening or spray-on no-stick oil. Do not use butter (it burns) or vegetable oil (it bakes to a sticky residue that is hard to clean).

Mixing: When directions tell you to cream the shortening and sugar, be sure to do this thoroughly: work the butter or other shortening against the side of the bowl until it is smooth and softened, then incorporate the sugar, blending until the mixture is fluffy. (If you are doing this by hand, it is possible to convince yourself that you will burn up as many calories making the cookies as you will consume by eating them.) Once the flour is added, the dough should be mixed well, but not beaten at length for this will toughen the cookies. Do not allow the dough to become too warm. If the dough seems sticky, refrigerate it rather than add more flour. Excessive flour is the main culprit in producing hard, dry cookies.

Shaping and rolling: The cookies in this book come in different shapes and sizes.

Bar cookies are generally made from a batter that is spread in a pan, then baked, cooled, and often stored right in the pan. In this way they are the simplest of cookies, requiring little handling.

Drop cookies are pushed, a rounded teaspoonful at a time, onto a cool cookie sheet. (Many bakers chill the dough and even chill the cookie sheets ahead of time.) Drop cookies usually spread as they bake, so be sure to allow about 2 inches between mounds of dough.

Molded cookies are made from a stiff dough that is formed by hand into little balls, crescents, canes, and other shapes, or forced through a cookie press. Handle the dough as little as possible and keep it chilled.

Rolled cookies are made from dough that is chilled briefly (about 20 minutes) and divided into two or three portions that are easy to work with. To avoid incorporating too much flour into the dough, roll it out on a pastry cloth rubbed lightly with flour. Dip the cookie cutters into flour (knocking off any excess) so that the edges won't stick. The thinner the dough, the more delicate and crisp the cookie. Cut-out cookies destined for hanging on the Christmas tree should be kept fairly thick. Poke a hole for string into the unbaked cookie, and insert small pieces of paper (not plastic) straw to keep the hole from baking shut. Be sure that all the cookies on a given cookie sheet are of the same thickness, to insure even baking. Scraps from rolling may be gathered, chilled, and rerolled, although cookies cut from scraps will not be quite as tender as those from the initial rolling.

After cutting or shaping cookies, put them on prepared cookie sheets and slip them into the freezer for a few minutes to help them hold their shape when they are baked. (This also seems to make cookies flakier.)

Baking: Be sure to preheat the oven; if the temperature is too low, cookies will melt before they begin to hold their shape. Most cookies bake at about 350°F, considered a "medium" oven temperature. If you don't trust your oven's thermostat, an inexpensive oven thermometer will give you a second opinion. It is best to bake one pan of cookies at a time, using the middle oven rack. If you occupy two oven racks, cookies on the top sheet may have brown tops and pale undersides while those on the bottom sheet have underdone tops and burnt bottoms, due to impaired heat circulation. If time is of the essence, bake two pans at once, but switch them from top to bottom halfway through baking. Many bakers also advise turning the cookie sheets front to back halfway through baking. Convection ovens tend to bake cookies faster and brown them more evenly; you may want to set the temperature a bit lower. Large cookie sheets may not fit into a convection oven.

Cooling: Using a metal spatula, remove cookies from the cookie sheet at once, unless directed otherwise, and place them gently on wire cooling racks. Do not pile cookies on top of each other. If you do not have enough space on the cooling racks, putting the cookies on plain brown paper grocery bags works well. Cool thoroughly before decorating, storing, or freezing.

Decorating: Cut-out cookies may be sprinkled with colored sugar or other decorations before baking. Brushing the cookies lightly with beaten egg white thinned with a few drops of water will help the sprinkles to adhere, but it is not essential. Most cookies are decorated after baking and cooling. Use a knife or short-bladed spatula to apply the frosting. Most frostings will hold up well in the refrigerator, covered, and may be restored to proper spreading consistency with a few drops of hot water, so it is not necessary to frost every cookie at once. (It is easier to store unfrosted cookies, for they can be stacked.)

STORING AND FREEZING COOKIES

Cookies that are brought home from the cookie exchange can be saved in the freezer. Because most cookies freeze well and thaw quickly, platefuls of assorted cookies can simply be covered well with plastic wrap or aluminum foil and popped into the freezer, to be brought out when company walks in the front door. (Placing unwrapped and unfrosted cookies in a 300°F oven for a few minutes will restore crispness.) You can make your own freezer "vacuum pack": place cookies in a Ziploc bag, seal almost completely, and insert a straw in the corner and use it to suck out the air. Three months in the freezer is about the maximum time before cookies begin to lose flavor.

For short-term storage at room temperature, place cooled cookies in a container with a snug lid. Be sure to separate crisp and soft cookies so their respective textures will be preserved. Place layers of waxed paper between soft cookies, frosted cookies, very delicate cookies, or bars when storing or freezing them. Store soft cookies in containers with tight lids to retain moisture. Add an apple slice if necessary to add humidity. Store crisp cookies in a container with a loose-fitting lid. Well packed, your homemade cookies will keep fresh in the kitchen for about a week.

TRANSPORTING AND MAILING COOKIES

Cookies can be carried by hand in rigid containers. Separate layers with sheets of waxed paper, and use additional lightly crumpled waxed paper on top to keep the contents from shifting. Cookies have also been known to outwit mauling machines in post offices. Bar cookies travel the best, for they can be packed nearly solidly into a container. Use a heavy cardboard box or metal coffee can. Use crumpled aluminum foil for packing and cushioning (it's expensive, but it works). But it is unreasonable to expect fragile or delicately frosted cookies to survive much handling at all. Those cookies are best eaten within walking distance of your kitchen.

2. CLASSIC COOKIES:

Family Favorites to Make
Year-Round

BEST-EVER
CHOCOLATE CHIP COOKIES

2 cups flour
1 teaspoon baking soda
1 teaspoon salt
1 cup butter, softened
3/4 cup sugar
1 cup brown sugar, firmly
  packed

1 teaspoon vanilla
2 eggs
12 ounces (2 cups) chocolate chips
1 cup chopped macadamia nuts

Combine flour, baking soda, and salt, and set aside. In a large bowl cream butter and sugars, beating until smooth. Add vanilla and beat in eggs. Gradually add flour mixture and blend well. Stir in chips and nuts. Drop by teaspoonfuls onto ungreased cookie sheets. Bake for 8 to 10 minutes at 375°F. MAKES ABOUT 40.

JACKIE ROGERS

CHOCOLATE CHIP COOKIES

1 cup sweet butter
3/4 cup sugar
3/4 cup brown sugar,
  firmly packed
1 teaspoon vanilla
2 eggs

2 1/4 cups flour
1 teaspoon baking soda
1/2 teaspoon salt
1 to 2 cups chocolate
  chips, as desired
3/4 cup chopped walnuts

Cream butter and sugars until fluffy. Add vanilla and eggs, and beat well. Add flour, baking soda, and salt, and mix well. Stir in chocolate chips and walnuts. Drop by teaspoonfuls onto ungreased cookie sheets, and bake at 375°F until golden brown. Cool on rack. MAKES ABOUT 40.

SUSAN MAHNKE PEERY

CRISPY
CHOCOLATE CHIP COOKIES

2 1/4 cups sifted flour
1 teaspoon baking soda
1 teaspoon salt
1/2 cup butter, softened
1/2 cup vegetable shortening
3/4 cup sugar
3/4 cup light brown sugar, firmly packed

1 teaspoon vanilla
2 tablespoons water
2 eggs
2 cups semi-sweet chocolate chips
1 cup chopped walnuts

Combine flour, baking soda, and salt, and set aside. Combine butter, shortening, both sugars, vanilla, and water in large mixing bowl and beat until creamy. Beat in eggs one at a time and mix until light. Add dry ingredients slowly and mix well. Stir in chocolate chips and chopped nuts. Drop by rounded teaspoonfuls onto lightly greased cookie sheets. Bake at 350°F for 10 to 12 minutes. MAKES 4 DOZEN.

NANCY PLATTS: *"This is a variation of a well-known recipe. It makes a larger, flatter, crispier cookie."*

SCRUNCHIES

1 cup butter
1 1/4 cups brown sugar, firmly packed
2 tablespoons milk
1 egg
3/4 cup salted or Spanish peanuts

3/4 cup chocolate chips
1 3/4 cups flour
1/4 teaspoon baking soda
2 teaspoons baking powder
1/4 teaspoon salt (optional)

Blend butter and sugar. Beat in milk and egg. Add peanuts and chips. Chill for 10 minutes. Sift dry ingredients together and add to chilled mixture. Drop by teaspoonfuls onto greased cookie sheets. Bake at 375°F for about 8 to 10 minutes. MAKES 5 DOZEN.

ELEANOR HOMEYER: *"This recipe came from a Canadian friend. It makes a variation of Toll House cookies."*

HERMITS

1/2 cup margarine
1 1/2 cups sugar
3 eggs, beaten
1/2 cup molasses
3 cups flour

1 teaspoon baking soda
1/2 teaspoon ground
  cloves
1/2 teaspoon nutmeg
1 teaspoon cinnamon
1 cup chopped raisins

Cream margarine and sugar. Add eggs and mix well. Add molasses. Add flour, baking soda, cloves, nutmeg, and cinnamon. Mix thoroughly. Stir in raisins. Chill dough for several hours. Drop by rounded teaspoonfuls onto greased cookie sheets, or pat out a small amount of dough by hand and cut with cookie cutters (resist adding too much extra flour, and do not roll with rolling pin). Bake at 375°F for 8 to 10 minutes. Do not overbake—cookies are best when chewy. MAKES ABOUT 4 DOZEN.

DORIS MORSE

DOUBLE GINGERSNAPS

1 1/2 cups butter or margarine
2 cups sugar
2 eggs
1/2 cup molasses
4 cups flour

2 teaspoons baking soda
2 teaspoons cinnamon
2 teaspoons ground cloves
4 teaspoons ground ginger
Sugar for rolling

Cream butter or margarine and sugar. Add eggs and molasses and blend well. Sift dry ingredients together. Add half of dry mixture to creamed mixture and blend with mixer. Add remaining half and blend by hand. Chill dough for several hours. At this point, you may bake whatever portion of the dough you desire, and refrigerate or freeze the remainder. (Dough keeps in the refrigerator, well covered, for at least a week. To freeze, wrap dough well in plastic or foil.) To bake, pull off pieces of dough to make balls the size of a walnut. Roll the balls in sugar and place on ungreased cookie sheets. Bake at 350°F for 15 to 18 minutes. Balls will flatten out and tops will be crackled. MAKES 5 TO 6 DOZEN. (Recipe may be halved or doubled.)

JODY SAVILLE

GINGER COOKIES

3/4 cup butter
1 cup brown sugar, firmly
  packed
1 egg
1/4 cup molasses
2 cups plus 1 tablespoon
  flour

2 teaspoons baking soda
1/4 teaspoon salt
1 teaspoon ground ginger
  (more to taste)
1 teaspoon cinnamon
Sugar for rolling

Cream butter and brown sugar. Add egg and molasses, and mix well. Combine flour, baking soda, salt, ginger, and cinnamon, and add to creamed mixture. Roll in balls and dip in sugar. Place on lightly greased cookie sheets and bake for 10 to 12 minutes at 375°F. MAKES ABOUT 4 DOZEN.

LUCILLE BILLINGS: *"I got this recipe from my sister-in-law, Glenna Adams of Cape Elizabeth, Maine. She had used it for years, and I've been using it for 18 years. It is one of my family's favorite cookies."*

PEANUT BUTTER COOKIES

1/2 cup butter
1/2 cup chunky peanut
  butter
1/2 cup sugar
1/2 cup brown sugar,
  firmly packed

1 egg
1 1/4 cups flour
1/2 teaspoon baking
  powder
1/2 teaspoon baking soda
1/4 teaspoon salt

Cream butter, peanut butter, and sugars until light. Add egg and mix well. Blend all dry ingredients and add to butter mixture. Mix well. Chill for 1 hour. Roll dough into 1" balls, and place 2" apart on lightly greased cookie sheets. Use a fork to flatten with crisscross pattern. Sprinkle with a bit of granulated sugar, if desired. Bake at 375°F for 10 to 12 minutes. MAKES ABOUT 36.

SUSAN MAHNKE PEERY: *"I often add a cup of chocolate chips to the recipe. Perfect with a glass of milk."*

PEANUT BLOSSOMS

1/2 cup butter
1/2 cup peanut butter,
  chunky or smooth
1/2 cup sugar
1/2 cup brown sugar,
  firmly packed
1 egg
2 tablespoons milk

1 teaspoon vanilla
1 3/4 cups flour
1 teaspoon baking soda
1/2 teaspoon salt
Sugar for rolling
Chocolate kisses or chocolate chips for topping

Cream butter, peanut butter, and sugars. Add egg and beat well. Add milk and vanilla. Stir in flour, baking soda, and salt. Mix well. Chill if necessary for handling. Form into 1" balls and roll in sugar. Place one chocolate kiss or several chocolate chips on top of each ball and press in firmly. Bake at 375°F for 10 to 12 minutes, until golden brown. Cool on rack. MAKES ABOUT 4 DOZEN.

MARGARET MAHNKE

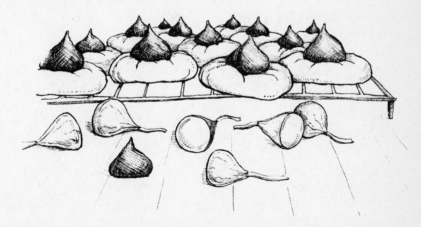

SAND TARTS

1 cup butter
1 1/4 cups sugar
1 egg
2 cups flour
1/4 cup finely chopped
  walnuts

2 teaspoons cinnamon
1 egg white, slightly
  beaten

Cream butter and gradually add 1 cup of the sugar, creaming well. Blend in egg. Gradually add flour, mixing well. If necessary, chill for easier handling. Combine remaining 1/4 cup of the sugar, walnuts, and cinnamon. Roll out half of dough on a floured surface and cut into 2" squares, or use cookie cutters for special shapes. Brush with egg white. Sprinkle with half of the sugar-nut mixture. Repeat with remaining dough and topping. Place on ungreased cookie sheets. Bake at 350°F for 8 to 10 minutes, until lightly browned. MAKES 6 DOZEN.

PARKY WAUGH: *"This is my grandmother's recipe. For the most tasty, light cookies, roll the dough as thinly as possible."*

SNICKERDOODLES

1 cup butter	1 teaspoon baking soda
1 1/2 cups sugar	1/4 teaspoon salt
2 eggs	1 cup raisins (optional)
2 3/4 cups flour	2 tablespoons sugar
2 teaspoons cream of tar- tar	2 teaspoons cinnamon

Mix butter, 1 1/2 cups sugar, and eggs. Blend flour, cream of tartar, baking soda, and salt. Stir into butter mixture. Add raisins if desired. Roll into 1" balls. Mix 2 tablespoons sugar with cinnamon and roll cookie balls in this mixture. Place 2" apart on ungreased cookie sheets. Bake at 400°F for 8 to 10 minutes. (Don't overcook: these are best when soft. They puff up at first, then flatten out.) MAKES 5 TO 6 DOZEN.

JACKIE FITZPATRICK

THUMBPRINT COOKIES

3/4 cup butter
1/2 cup brown sugar,
  firmly packed
1 egg, separated
1/2 teaspoon vanilla

1 1/3 cups flour
1/4 teaspoon salt
Chopped nuts
Fruit jam

Cream butter and sugar. Add egg yolk and vanilla. Add flour and salt. Mix well. Add a bit more flour if dough is too sticky. Shape dough into 1" balls. Beat egg white until foamy. Roll cookie balls in egg white, then in chopped nuts. Place 1" apart on greased cookie sheets. Press hole in center of each cookie. Bake for 8 to 10 minutes at 350°, until golden. Cool on rack, then place jam in center of each cookie. MAKES 3 DOZEN.

GERI KORTEN: *"These cookies freeze easily. Don't add the jam until you're ready to serve them."*

OATMEAL LACE COOKIES

1 cup butter
1 1/2 cups dark brown
   sugar, firmly packed
2 1/4 cups quick oats

1/2 teaspoon salt
3 tablespoons flour
1 teaspoon vanilla
1 egg, slightly beaten

In a saucepan, melt butter. Add sugar and stir until dissolved. Pour butter mixture over oats and mix. Let stand at room temperature for 8 hours or overnight. Add salt, flour, vanilla, and egg to oats mixture and combine well. Drop by small spoonfuls onto well-greased cookie sheets, allowing room for cookies to spread. Bake, 1 sheet at a time, for 5 to 7 minutes at 375°F. Let stand about 30 seconds before removing to cooling rack. MAKES 3 TO 4 DOZEN.

JACKIE ROGERS

OATMEAL MOLASSES COOKIES

1/2 cup butter or margarine
1 cup sugar
2 eggs
6 tablespoons molasses
1 3/4 cups flour
1 teaspoon baking soda

1 teaspoon salt
1 teaspoon cinnamon
2 cups old-fashioned oats
1 cup chopped nuts
1/2 cup raisins

Cream butter and sugar. Add eggs and molasses. Sift flour, baking soda, salt, and cinnamon together, and add to creamed mixture. Mix well. Stir in oats, nuts, and raisins. Drop onto greased cookie sheets and bake at 400°F for 8 to 10 minutes. MAKES ABOUT 4 DOZEN.

> LUCILLE BILLINGS: *"These cookies are delicious and nutritious, great for after-school snacks or to pack in lunch boxes. My mother got the recipe from one of her friends and passed it along to me several years ago."*

LEMON SUGAR COOKIES

2 3/4 cups flour
2 teaspoons baking
  powder
1/4 teaspoon salt
1 cup butter
2 cups sugar

2 eggs
2 teaspoons grated lemon
  rind
3 tablespoons lemon juice
1 cup quick oats

Sift together flour, baking powder, and salt. In large bowl, cream butter and sugar. Add eggs, beating well. Beat in lemon rind and juice. Gradually add flour mixture, then stir in oats. Chill dough thoroughly (at least 2 hours). Roll level tablespoonfuls of dough into balls and place on greased cookie sheets, allowing room for cookies to spread. Using a flat-bottomed glass or custard cup that has been greased and dipped in sugar, flatten each ball to 1/4" thickness (dip the glass in sugar each time). Bake at 375°F until lightly browned around the edges, about 8 to 10 minutes. Cool for one minute, then carefully remove from cookie sheets and cool on racks. MAKES 4 DOZEN.

SUSAN MAHNKE PEERY: *"This recipe is on a yellowed newspaper clipping that I've had for years. The cookies are delicate and delicious."*

COCONUT OATMEAL COOKIES

1 cup sugar
1 cup brown sugar, firmly
  packed
1 cup shredded coconut
1 cup sifted flour
1 teaspoon baking soda

1 teaspoon salt
2 eggs, beaten
1/2 cup butter and 1/2 cup
  margarine, melted
1 teaspoon vanilla
4 cups rolled oats

Mix together sugars, coconut, flour, baking soda, and salt. Add beaten eggs, butter and margarine, and vanilla. Stir in rolled oats. Drop by teaspoonfuls onto lightly greased cookie sheets and bake at 375°F for 10 to 12 minutes. MAKES 4 TO 5 DOZEN.

LAUREL GABEL: *"I got this recipe years ago from my mother-in-law."*

MOXIE COOKIES

1/2 cup butter
1 cup sugar
1 egg
1/2 teaspoon almond
  extract
1 cup flour

1 teaspoon baking powder
1/4 teaspoon salt
3/4 cup oatmeal
1 egg white, lightly beaten
Sugar-cinnamon mixture

Cream butter and sugar. Add egg and almond extract. Add flour, baking powder, and salt. Stir in oatmeal. Chill dough and roll out fairly thin. Cut into desired shapes with cookie cutters. Brush cookies with egg white and sprinkle with sugar-cinnamon mixture. Bake on lightly greased cookie sheets at 350°F for 8 to 10 minutes. MAKES ABOUT 3 DOZEN.

SUSAN MAHNKE PEERY: *"This cookie was a kitchen experiment in celebration of the adoption of our dog, Moxie, in 1977. (It has nothing at all to do with the soft drink called Moxie!) The dog Moxie is alive and well at this writing, probably due to all the cookies he's begged over the years."*

MERINGUE KISSES

4 egg whites
1 cup sugar

1 cup miniature chocolate chips or 1 cup chopped nuts

In a glass bowl, beat the egg whites until foamy. Continue to beat while gradually adding sugar. Beat until stiff. Fold in chips or nuts. Drop by teaspoonfuls onto greased cookie sheets. Place in 375°F oven and immediately turn oven off. Let kisses remain in oven for 1 1/2 to 2 hours. Do not open oven door until 1 1/2 hours have passed. MAKES ABOUT 60.

ANN BEVILACQUA

SESAME SEED COOKIES

2 cups flour
3/4 cup sugar
1 1/2 teaspoons baking powder
1/4 teaspoon salt
2/3 cup butter

2 egg yolks
1/4 cup milk
1 teaspoon vanilla
1/3 cup toasted sesame seeds

Sift dry ingredients into a bowl. Cut in butter with pastry blender. Add egg yolks, milk, and vanilla. Mix with a fork, then knead until smooth. Shape tablespoonfuls of dough into ovals. Roll in sesame seeds and place on greased cookie sheets. Bake at 375°F for 15 to 20 minutes. MAKES ABOUT 30 COOKIES.

CHRIS COPPOLINO (*Mary's mother*)

AUNT LIZZIE'S SLUGS

1 cup butter
1 1/2 cups sugar
3 eggs
1 cup chopped walnuts
1 cup raisins

1 teaspoon vanilla
1 teaspoon baking soda
2 tablespoons hot water
1 teaspoon baking powder
3 cups flour

Cream butter and sugar. Add eggs, walnuts, raisins, and vanilla. Dissolve baking soda in hot water and add to mixture. Add baking powder and flour, and mix well. Drop by teaspoonfuls onto greased cookie sheet. Bake at 350°F for 8 to 10 minutes, until lightly browned. MAKES 5 TO 6 DOZEN.

ELEANOR HOMEYER: *"This recipe came from a church women's cookbook. The person who submitted it to that cookbook got it from a Swedish friend. I often get requests to bring these cookies to picnics."*

LEMON-COCONUT COOKIES

1/2 cup butter
3/4 cup brown sugar,
  firmly packed
1 egg
Juice and grated rind of
  1/2 lemon

1/2 cup whole-wheat flour
1/2 cup all-purpose flour
1/2 teaspoon baking soda
1/4 teaspoon salt
3/4 cup shredded coconut
1/2 cup chopped walnuts

Cream butter and sugar. Add egg, lemon juice, and lemon rind. Mix flours, baking soda, and salt, and add to butter mixture. Stir in coconut and walnuts. Drop by teaspoonfuls onto lightly greased cookie sheets and bake at 350°F for about 10 minutes, until golden. MAKES ABOUT 36.

SUSAN MAHNKE PEERY

HONEY SPICE COOKIES

3/4 cup butter, softened
3/4 cup sugar
1/4 cup honey
1 egg
2 cups flour
1/2 teaspoon salt
1/2 teaspoon baking soda

1/2 teaspoon freshly grated nutmeg
1/4 teaspoon ground cloves
1/2 teaspoon orange extract

Cream butter and sugar. Add honey and egg, and mix well. Add flour, salt, baking soda, nutmeg, and cloves, and blend. Add orange extract and mix well. Drop by rounded teaspoonfuls onto ungreased cookie sheets, allowing 2″ between cookies. Bake at 375°F for 10 minutes, until edges are lightly browned. Transfer cookies to wire racks to cool. While still warm, frost with a glaze made by combining 1 cup confectioners' sugar, 2 tablespoons milk, and 2 teaspoons grated orange peel. MAKES 35 TO 40.

SUSAN MAHNKE PEERY

PUMPKIN COOKIES

2 cups flour
1 teaspoon cinnamon
1 teaspoon baking soda
1 teaspoon baking powder
1/2 teaspoon salt
1 cup butter, or 1/2 cup
  butter and 1/2 cup mar-
  garine

1 cup sugar
1 egg
1 teaspoon vanilla
1 cup cooked pumpkin,
  mashed (canned may be
  used)
1/2 cup raisins
1/2 cup nuts, chopped

Frosting:

3 tablespoons butter
1/2 cup brown sugar,
  firmly packed

1 cup confectioners' sugar
3 tablespoons milk
3/4 teaspoon vanilla

Sift together flour, cinnamon, baking soda, baking powder, and salt. Cream butter and sugar. Add egg, vanilla, and pumpkin. Then add raisins and nuts. Fold in flour mixture. Drop by teaspoonfuls onto ungreased cookie sheets and bake at 350°F for 15 minutes. Cool cookies on rack.

To prepare frosting: Melt butter; add sugars, milk, and vanilla. Beat well. Spread on cooled cookies. MAKES 3 TO 4 DOZEN.

JUDY PATENAUDE

GOLDEN CARROT COOKIES

1 cup shortening (half
   butter, half margarine)
3/4 cup sugar
2 eggs
1 cup cooked and mashed
   carrots

2 cups sifted flour
2 teaspoons baking
   powder
1/2 teaspoon salt
3/4 cup shredded coconut
1 teaspoon vanilla

Frosting:

2 cups confectioners'
   sugar
Dash of salt
4 teaspoons grated orange
   rind

6 tablespoons soft butter
Orange juice to reach
   spreading consistency

Cream shortening and sugar. Add eggs and carrots. Mix well. Add remaining ingredients in order given. Drop teaspoonfuls of dough on greased cookie sheets and bake at 375°F for 8 to 10 minutes. Cool on rack.

To prepare frosting: Mix sugar, salt, orange rind, and butter with a fork. Add orange juice and mix with electric mixer until smooth. Spread on cooled cookies. MAKES 4 DOZEN.

JEAN DE LONGCHAMP

CALIFORNIA FIG COOKIES

1 cup (1/2 pound) chopped
  golden or black figs
1/3 cup water
1 cup butter
1/2 cup sugar
1/2 cup brown sugar,
  firmly packed
1 egg

1 teaspoon vanilla
2 cups flour
2 teaspoons baking
  powder
1/2 teaspoon salt
Walnut or pecan halves
  (optional)

Cook figs in water, stirring frequently, until thickened, about 5 minutes. Set aside to cool. Beat butter with both sugars until light and fluffy. Beat in egg and vanilla. Sift together flour, baking powder, and salt. Mix into creamed mixture. Stir in cooled figs. Drop by teaspoonfuls about 2″ apart onto lightly greased cookie sheets. Press a nut half on top of each cookie if desired. Bake at 375°F for 10 to 12 minutes, until lightly browned. Cool cookies on rack. MAKES 4 DOZEN.

LUCY CORTICELLI

POTATO CHIP COOKIES

1 pound butter
1 cup sugar
3 cups sifted flour
2 cups crushed potato
  chips

1 cup chopped nuts
1 teaspoon vanilla
Confectioners' sugar

Cream butter. Add sugar and beat until light and fluffy. Stir in flour. Mix well. Add potato chips, nuts, and vanilla. Roll into balls about 3/4″ in diameter. Place on ungreased cookie sheets and bake at 325°F for 20 minutes. When cool, sprinkle with confectioners' sugar. MAKES 7 DOZEN.

ROSALEE OAKLEY: *"These cookies taste like Russian tea cakes."*

WEIRD WONDERS

3 egg whites
1 cup sugar
1/8 teaspoon salt
1 teaspoon vanilla
1 1/2 cups Peanut Butter
   Captain Crunch cereal

1/2 cup chopped walnuts
1 cup chocolate chips
1 cup shredded coconut

Preheat oven to 350°F. In a large bowl, beat egg whites until foamy. Gradually add sugar and salt. Beat until stiff. Add vanilla. Gently fold in cereal, nuts, chocolate, and coconut. Line a jelly-roll pan with foil and drop teaspoonfuls of batter onto the foil (they will not spread). Place in oven and immediately turn oven off. Leave in oven, with door shut, for 3 hours. Remove and place in covered container. MAKES 4 DOZEN.

WINNIE ODELL

CHEESE KRISPIES

3/4 cup butter, softened
9 ounces sharp cheddar
  cheese, grated
1 1/2 cups sifted flour

1/2 teaspoon salt
1/2 to 1 teaspoon Tabasco
  sauce
3 cups Rice Krispies cereal

Cream butter and cheese well. Gradually add flour, salt, and Tabasco. Knead with fingers until well blended. Add Rice Krispies and knead together. Roll into 1" balls, place on ungreased cookie sheets, and press with a fork until cookies are round and about 1/4" thick. Bake at 400°F for about 10 minutes. Cool on rack. Store in a sealed tin. MAKES ABOUT 50.

> ROSALEE OAKLEY: *"This* unsweet *cookie is very enjoyable. The recipe is from Mrs. Isaac N. Smith, Jr., who got it from a collection of recipes compiled by the Junior League of Charleston, West Virginia."*

YOUR BASIC COOKIES:
THEME AND VARIATIONS

2 cups flour
1/4 teaspoon salt
1 teaspoon baking powder
3/4 cup butter

1 cup sugar (half brown, if
  desired)
1 egg
1 teaspoon vanilla

Mix flour, salt, and baking powder. Cream butter and sugar; add egg and vanilla. Add flour mixture. Drop by teaspoonfuls onto greased cookie sheets and bake at 350°F for about 10 minutes. MAKES ABOUT 36.

Variations:

1. Roll dough into 3/4" balls and flatten as thin as possible. Sprinkle with sesame seeds and flatten a little more.

2. Add 1 cup shredded coconut (more or less to taste) to basic recipe. Roll into balls and flatten.

3. Add currants or raisins (about 1 cup) to variation 2.

4. Roll into balls and top with a walnut or pecan before baking.

5. Butter tiny cupcake tins and press basic cookie dough into wells as thinly as possible. Fill as desired; one suggestion is Apricot Filling: boil dried apricots in water to cover for about 10 minutes, until soft. Drain off most of the water; add brown sugar to taste, and purée in blender. Cool, then add chopped nuts. Place filling in dough-lined pans and bake at 350°F for about 10 minutes, until dough is lightly browned.

6. Improvise: Add chocolate bits, raisins, grated orange or lemon rind, anything you think might work.

MICHELINA PRENCIPE: *"This recipe was given to me by a friend, June Palatini, of Lodi, New Jersey. A good tip from June: If you run out of brown sugar, don't bother going to the store. Just mix some molasses with white sugar, and you'll get 'reconstituted' brown sugar."*

3. REFRIGERATOR
COOKIES

PINWHEELS

2/3 cup butter or marga-
  rine
1 cup sugar
2 egg yolks
1 teaspoon vanilla
6 tablespoons milk
3 cups flour (cake flour
  may be used)

1 teaspoon salt
1 teaspoon baking powder
2 cups ground walnuts
2 ounces baking choco-
  late, melted

Cream butter and sugar. Add egg yolks and beat. Add vanilla and milk. Sift together flour, salt, and baking powder and add to butter mixture. Add the ground nuts. Divide dough into two parts. Add the melted chocolate to
one part. Chill both halves for at least an hour. Roll out
both parts to similarly shaped rectangles, and place chocolate dough on top of the plain dough. Press together lightly
with a rolling pin. Roll up like a jelly roll to make a log
about 2″ in diameter. Wrap in waxed paper and chill until
firm. Slice 1/8″ thick. Bake on greased cookie sheets at
350°F for 8 to 10 minutes. MAKES ABOUT 60.

LOUISE BOLLES: *"This recipe came from a cookbook I've
had for 26 years. The book is battered, without a cover,
and missing half the index, but still a great reference.
This recipe is a favorite."*

DATE PINWHEELS

1/2 cup butter
1/2 cup brown sugar,
  firmly packed
1/2 cup sugar

1 egg
2 cups flour
1/2 teaspoon baking soda
1/4 teaspoon salt

Filling:

1/2 pound chopped dates
1/3 cup water

1/2 cup sugar
1/4 cup chopped walnuts

To make filling: Combine dates, water, sugar, and walnuts in a heavy saucepan. Cook for 5 minutes over medium heat, stirring frequently. Cool.

To make dough: Cream butter and sugars. Add egg and mix well. Sift the flour with soda and salt and combine with the creamed mixture. Roll out to a narrow rectangle. Spread with the date filling and roll up from the long side, jelly-roll fashion. (Or make two shorter rolls.) Refrigerate for at least several hours. Cut into thin slices and place on greased cookie sheets. Bake at 400°F for 10 to 12 minutes. MAKES ABOUT 36, DEPENDING ON THICKNESS OF SLICES.

MARY BEVILACQUA

BROWN SUGAR
REFRIGERATOR COOKIES

1/2 cup butter
1/2 cup margarine
2 cups brown sugar,
  firmly packed
2 eggs
3 cups flour
1/2 teaspoon baking soda

1 teaspoon cream of tartar
1/2 teaspoon freshly
  grated nutmeg
1 tablespoon water
1 teaspoon vanilla

Cream butter, margarine, and brown sugar until fluffy. Add eggs and beat well. Combine dry ingredients and add to butter mixture. Add water and vanilla and mix. Divide dough into two rolls and wrap in waxed paper. Chill for several hours or overnight. Slice 1/4" thick and place 2" apart on ungreased cookie sheets. Bake at 350°F for 10 to 12 minutes, until golden brown. MAKES ABOUT 4 1/2 DOZEN.

SUSAN MAHNKE PEERY: *"You can bake one roll and freeze the other, if you prefer. (Wrap the roll securely in plastic wrap or foil for freezing.) The nutmeg in these cookies makes them special."*

CRISP OATMEAL COOKIES

1 cup butter or margarine
1/2 cup sugar
1 cup brown sugar, firmly
  packed
2 eggs, beaten
1 teaspoon vanilla

1 1/2 cups flour
1 teaspoon salt
1 teaspoon baking soda
3 cups oatmeal
1/2 cup nuts, chopped

Cream butter and sugars. Add eggs and vanilla. Sift dry ingredients and add to butter mixture. Add oats and nuts and mix well. Shape into two rolls 2" in diameter and wrap in plastic wrap. Refrigerate for several hours, until firm. Slice about 1/4" thick and bake on lightly greased cookie sheets at 350°F for 10 to 12 minutes. MAKES 5 DOZEN.

MARY BEVILACQUA

PECAN CHARMS

1 cup butter or margarine
1 cup sugar
2 tablespoons milk
1 teaspoon vanilla

3 cups flour
1/2 teaspoon salt
1 1/2 cups finely chopped
  pecans

Beat butter and sugar until light. Blend in milk and vanilla. Add flour, salt, and pecans, and mix well. Shape dough into two rolls, each about 2″ in diameter. Wrap securely and chill for several hours or overnight. Cut into 1/4″ slices and place on ungreased cookie sheets. Bake at 375°F for 10 to 12 minutes, until lightly browned on edges. MAKES ABOUT 7 DOZEN.

MAUREEN ZOCK: *"These cookies are crisp and tasty, and are perfect for giving, because they do not lose their shape or break easily. Delicious with a cup of English Breakfast tea."*

VANILLA REFRIGERATOR COOKIES

1 1/2 cups vegetable
  shortening
1 cup sugar
2 cups brown sugar,
  firmly packed
3 eggs

4 1/2 cups flour
1 teaspoon baking soda
1 teaspoon cinnamon
1 teaspoon salt
8 ounces finely chopped
  walnuts

Cream shortening and sugars in large mixing bowl. Add eggs one at a time, beating after each one. Sift together dry ingredients and add to butter mixture. Stir in chopped nuts. Shape dough into two rolls, each about 2″ in diameter, and wrap in plastic or foil. Refrigerate or freeze for several hours or overnight. Slice thinly and place on lightly greased cookie sheets. Bake at 375°F for about 8 minutes. MAKES 6 TO 8 DOZEN.

NANCY PLATTS: *"These are called 'vanilla' cookies, but there is no vanilla in them. The combination of brown sugar and cinnamon gives them a slight butterscotch flavor. If you freeze the dough, the cookies can be sliced thinner and will be more crisp."*

CHOCOLATE REFRIGERATOR COOKIES

◆————————————————————————————◆

1 cup plus 2 tablespoons
   flour
3 tablespoons cocoa
1/2 cup butter, softened

6 tablespoons sugar
1 teaspoon vanilla
1/8 teaspoon salt
Slivered almonds

Mix flour and cocoa; set aside. Cream butter, sugar, vanilla, and salt until fluffy. Gradually add flour mixture. Shape dough into a 9″ roll. Wrap in plastic and chill for several hours or overnight. Cut in 1/4″ slices. Place 1″ apart on lightly greased cookie sheets. Press an almond sliver on each. Bake at 350°F for about 12 minutes. Cool on rack. MAKES ABOUT 36.

SUSAN MAHNKE PEERY

4. NO-BAKE AND FRIED COOKIES

DATE-NUT ROLLS

4 tablespoons butter
2 cups sugar
4 eggs
1 cup chopped dates
4 cups Rice Krispies cereal

1 cup walnuts, coarsely
  chopped
2 teaspoons vanilla
7 ounces shredded coco-
  nut

Melt butter in saucepan. Remove from heat and stir in sugar, eggs, and dates. Return to low heat and cook, stirring constantly, until mixture leaves the sides of the pan. Remove from heat. Add cereal, nuts, and vanilla. Mix well. Let cool until mixture can be handled, then form into finger-size logs about 2" long. Roll in coconut. Freeze or refrigerate. MAKES 4 DOZEN.

MARY BEVILACQUA

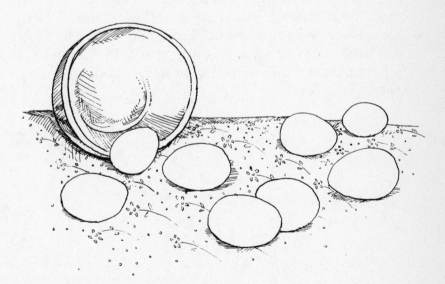

MARSHMALLOW MOSAICS

6 ounces semi-sweet choc-
  olate
2 eggs
1 teaspoon vanilla
One 10 1/2-ounce bag
  colored miniature marshmallows

1 1/2 cups finely chopped
  toasted nuts
2 cups graham cracker
  crumbs

Melt chocolate in double boiler over simmering water. Remove from heat. Beat in eggs and vanilla. Fold in marshmallows and 1 cup of the nuts. Combine graham cracker crumbs and remaining nuts. Cut 6 pieces of waxed paper in 12" lengths. Sprinkle the crumb mixture evenly over half of each piece, keeping the crumb side closest to you. Place spoonfuls of the marshmallow-chocolate mixture on top of the crumbs, dividing the mixture between the 6 pieces. Using the waxed paper as a roller, carefully shape each mixture into a log 1 1/2" to 2" thick. Twist the ends of the paper and refrigerate until the chocolate has hardened. Cut on a diagonal into 1/4" slices with a serrated knife. Rolls may also be frozen. MAKES 6 ROLLS, ABOUT 60 SLICES.

JACKIE FITZPATRICK

BOW COOKIES

3 eggs, well beaten
3 tablespoons sugar
1/2 teaspoon salt
1 tablespoon vanilla

3 cups flour
Oil for frying
Confectioners' sugar

Mix together eggs, sugar, salt, vanilla, and flour until well blended. Taking a small part of the dough at a time, roll out very thin and cut into strips about 6″ long and 1 1/2″ wide. Make a slit in the center and pull one side of the dough through the slit. Fry in oil until golden brown and drain on paper towels. Sprinkle with confectioners' sugar. MAKES 4 DOZEN.

CHRIS COPPOLINO

PEANUT BUTTER BALLS

1 cup butter
1 cup peanut butter,
  smooth or chunky
1 1/2 cups graham cracker
  crumbs

2 cups confectioners'
  sugar
8 ounces (1 1/4 cups)
  chocolate chips, melted
  over hot water

Melt butter and peanut butter together in a double boiler over simmering water. Mix in crumbs and sugar. Roll into balls and dip in melted chocolate. Place on waxed paper to harden. MAKES ABOUT 40.

NANCY COPPOLINO: *"These cookies are yummy, quick, and a great winter afternoon project with kids."*

BUCKEYE BALLS

1 1/2 cups peanut butter
1 pound confectioners'
  sugar
1/2 cup butter, softened
1 teaspoon vanilla

6 ounces (1 cup) chocolate
  chips
2 tablespoons vegetable
  shortening

Mix peanut butter (I prefer chunky), sugar, butter, and vanilla together in a bowl. Line a cookie sheet with waxed paper. Roll the cookie mixture into bite-size round balls. Place on cookie sheet and refrigerate for 1 hour. Then melt the chocolate chips with the vegetable shortening in double boiler over hot water. Using a toothpick, dip the balls into the melted chocolate, leaving the top quarter of each ball undipped. Return to cookie sheet to cool and allow chocolate to harden. Keep refrigerated until ready to serve.
MAKES ABOUT 5 DOZEN, DEPENDING ON SIZE.

> LUCY CORTICELLI: *"My husband usually makes these—they taste like Reese's Peanut Butter Cups. If any chocolate is left over, he throws a few pecans or walnuts into the pan and drops them by spoonfuls onto waxed paper, then refrigerates the clusters."*

NEBRASKA CHOCOLATE BALLS

1 pound confectioners'
   sugar
2 cups chunky peanut
   butter
1/2 cup butter, softened

3 1/2 cups Rice Krispies
   cereal
12 ounces (2 cups) choco-
   late chips

Mix sugar, peanut butter, butter, and cereal with fingers
and roll into walnut-size balls. Chill overnight. In a double boiler over hot water, melt the chocolate chips. Dip
each ball into the chocolate mixture. MAKES ABOUT 50.

WINNIE ODELL

COFFEE NUT BONBONS

2 1/2 cups walnuts
1 1/4 cups sugar

1/4 cup hot espresso
   coffee

In a food processor, blend nuts with sugar, then add 1/4
cup hot coffee and process until firmly mixed. Form into
little balls. Cover with icing made by combining 1 1/2
cup confectioners' sugar with 1/4 cup hot espresso coffee.
Decorate if desired with sugar-coated pecan halves or
candied fruit. MAKES ABOUT 30.

MONICA FORMAN

RUM BALLS

2 cups chocolate-wafer
  crumbs
1 cup confectioners' sugar
1 cup chopped nuts
2 tablespoons cocoa

3 tablespoons maple syrup
1/2 cup rum (approxi-
  mately)
Chocolate sprinkles or
  chopped nuts for rolling

Combine crumbs, sugar, nuts, cocoa, and maple syrup with enough rum to moisten. Form into balls and roll in chocolate sprinkles or chopped nuts. Refrigerate. Serve at room temperature for best flavor. MAKES 3 DOZEN.

LAUREL GABEL

FRUIT BALLS

1 cup dates
1 cup figs

2 cups walnuts
Sugar for rolling

Grind all ingredients except sugar. Mix well and form into 3/4" balls. Roll in sugar. Store in a covered container. MAKES ABOUT 48.

MARY BEVILACQUA: *"These are very nutritious! I got the recipe from a 'health-food' friend."*

PINK ALMOND PEARLS

8 ounces almond paste
1 cup sifted confectioners'
  sugar
2 tablespoons water
1/2 cup finely chopped
  seedless raisins

1/2 cup finely chopped
  dried apricots
1 teaspoon rum flavoring
1/2 teaspoon vanilla

Icing:
1 egg white
1/2 teaspoon white
  vinegar

1 3/4 cups confectioners'
  sugar
Red food coloring

Combine almond paste, confectioners' sugar, water, raisins, apricots, rum flavoring, and vanilla in a medium bowl. Mix with a fork to blend completely. Roll 1 teaspoonful at a time into small balls. Drop into pink icing. Lift out with a fork and hold over bowl to catch drips. Place on a rack over waxed paper. Let stand 2 to 3 hours, until icing is set. MAKES 4 DOZEN.

To prepare icing: Beat egg white in small bowl. Beat in vinegar and add confectioners' sugar. Continue beating with an electric mixer until icing becomes thick and fluffy. Tint pink with a drop or two of food coloring.

LAUREL GABEL

CHOCOLATE POODLES

◆————————————————————————◆

1/4 cup cocoa
2 cups sugar
1/2 cup butter
1/2 cup milk

1/2 cup peanut butter,
   smooth or chunky
1 teaspoon vanilla
4 to 5 cups oatmeal

Heat cocoa, sugar, butter, and milk. Bring to a boil and cook for 1 1/2 minutes. Remove from heat and stir in peanut butter, vanilla, and enough oats to give the mixture body. Drop by teaspoonfuls onto a cookie sheet lined with waxed paper. Refrigerate for 1 hour, until firm. MAKES ABOUT 40.

SUSAN MAHNKE PEERY: *"This recipe was clipped from a newspaper years ago."*

CHOCOLATE
ALMOND RAISIN CLUSTERS

◆————————————————————————◆

1 cup whole unskinned al-
  monds
2 cups (12 ounces) semi-
  sweet chocolate chips

1/2 cup raisins

Toast the almonds in a baking pan for 10 minutes at 350°F. Place the hot almonds in a bowl with the chocolate chips and stir until the chips are melted. Stir in the raisins and drop tablespoonfuls of the mixture onto a cookie sheet lined with waxed paper. Chill for 20 minutes, until hardened. Store covered in the refrigerator. MAKES ABOUT 24.

SUSAN MAHNKE PEERY

PRETZELS DIPPED IN
DARK OR WHITE CHOCOLATE

◆————————————————————————————◆

1 bag twisted, salted pretzels	1 pound dipping chocolate, white or dark (available at party-goods stores)

Melt chocolate over hot water in a double boiler. Dip pretzels until fully covered. Let excess chocolate drip back into pot. Cool on waxed paper. Store in refrigerator or freezer. MAKES ABOUT 40.

ANN BEVILACQUA: *"This is a great hostess gift at Christmas time or anytime!"*

BUTTERSCOTCH NOODLES

◆————————————————————————————◆

12 ounces butterscotch chips 1/2 cup peanut butter, smooth or chunky	1 large can Chinese noodles

Melt chips and peanut butter over simmering water in a double boiler. Remove from heat. Stir in noodles. Line a cookie sheet with waxed paper, and place spoonfuls of mixture on the paper. Refrigerate to firm. MAKES ABOUT 36.

ROSALEE OAKLEY

5. HEIRLOOM RECIPES:

Cookies That Immigrated
to America

MELOMAKAROUNA
(GREEK HONEY SPICE COOKIES)

◆━━━━━━━━━━━━━━━━━━━━━━━━━━━━━━━━━◆

1/2 cup butter, softened
1/4 cup vegetable oil
1/4 cup sugar
1 egg yolk
2 tablespoons orange juice
1 tablespoon lemon juice
2 1/4 cups flour

3/4 teaspoon baking
  powder
1/2 teaspoon cinnamon
1/4 cup milk
Honey Syrup *
2 tablespoons finely
  chopped walnuts

In a mixing bowl, cream butter, oil, and sugar until light. Beat in egg yolk and orange and lemon juices. Stir together flour, baking powder, and cinnamon. Add to creamed mixture alternately with milk, beating well after each addition. Using 1 tablespoon of dough for each cookie, shape in ovals about 2" long and 1 1/2" wide. Place on ungreased cookie sheets and bake at 325°F for 25 to 30 minutes. Remove from cookie sheet; cool on wire rack. Place waxed paper under racks. Dip cooled cookies in Honey Syrup and drain on rack. Sprinkle lightly with chopped walnuts. MAKES 3 DOZEN.

*Honey Syrup: In a saucepan, combine 1 cup sugar, 1/2 cup water, and 1/2 cup honey. Bring to boil; cook gently, uncovered, for 10 minutes. Remove from heat; keep warm for use.

> PARKY WAUGH: *"Make these cookies several days before eating, so they have time to absorb the honey syrup."*

MOROCCAN ALMOND ROLLS

2 1/4 cups sifted flour
1 cup butter

1/2 teaspoon salt
4 tablespoons ice water

Filling:
8 ounces almond paste
1 egg

2 tablespoons sugar
1/3 cup ground almonds

Place flour, butter, and salt in a mixing bowl. Cut in butter with a pastry blender until mixture is crumbly. Add water and mix well with a fork until moistened. Shape into a ball. Divide into three sections, wrap, and refrigerate for 1 hour. Meanwhile, prepare filling by mixing all ingredients together.

Remove dough from refrigerator, and roll out 1 section into a 12″ × 12″ square. Cut into 3″ squares. Place a small piece of filling at one corner of each small square and roll up diagonally. Repeat with remaining two sections of dough. Place rolled squares on ungreased cookie sheets and bake at 400°F for 10 to 12 minutes. MAKES 48.

MARY BEVILACQUA: *"I got this recipe from a former neighbor from Ohio. Her mother-in-law used these for a midwestern cookie exchange 25 years ago!"*

TAFTA'S FENECHIA

1/2 cup melted vegetable
  shortening
1/2 cup vegetable oil
1 cup milk
4 to 5 cups flour
4 teaspoons baking powder

Pinch of salt
1 1/2 cups chopped nuts
1 cup chopped dates
1 cup maple syrup

Combine vegetable shortening, oil, milk, flour, baking powder, and salt to make a dough. Add 1 cup of the chopped nuts. Break off small pieces of dough and fold 1 teaspoonful of dates in each. Place on a lightly greased cookie sheet. Bake for 30 to 35 minutes at 375°F. Remove from oven, and immediately pour 3/4 cup of the maple syrup over the cookies. When cookies are cool, brush them with the remaining 1/4 cup of syrup and top each cookie with a few of the reserved chopped nuts. MAKES ABOUT 48.

> JANET MEANY: *"This is an Albanian cookie recipe. If you don't have maple syrup, you can substitute simple-sugar syrup, made by boiling 1 part water to 2 parts sugar for 5 minutes."*

SWEDISH GINGER COOKIES

1 cup butter
1 1/2 cups sugar
1 egg
1 1/2 tablespoons grated
orange rind
2 tablespoons dark corn
syrup
1 tablespoon water

3 1/4 cups flour
2 teaspoons baking soda
2 teaspoons cinnamon
1 teaspoon ground ginger
(more to taste)
1/2 teaspoon ground
cloves

Cream butter and sugar until light. Add egg, orange rind, corn syrup, and water, and mix well. Sift together dry ingredients and add to butter mixture. Chill dough thoroughly. Roll out very thin, about 1/8", and cut with cookie cutters. Bake on ungreased cookie sheets at 350°F for 8 to 10 minutes. Do not overbake, or cookies will burn. MAKES 60.

MERLE PEERY: *"This recipe was given to me by Carol Hougas, whose son was born the same afternoon as my daughter Karen."*

FINNISH CHESTNUT FINGERS

6 tablespoons butter
1/4 cup sugar
1 egg yolk
1/2 cup chestnut purée
1/2 teaspoon vanilla
1 cup flour

1/4 teaspoon cinnamon
1/4 teaspoon salt
Sugar
3 ounces semi-sweet
  chocolate

Cream butter; add sugar and beat until fluffy. Add egg yolk and beat. Mix in chestnut purée and vanilla. Add flour, cinnamon, and salt, and mix well. Chill dough for easier handling. Roll scant teaspoonfuls of dough into 2 1/2" fingers. Place on greased cookie sheets and sprinkle with sugar. Bake at 300°F for 20 minutes, until slightly browned. Cool on rack. Melt chocolate; dip one end of each cookie finger into the melted chocolate. Place on wax paper to harden. MAKES ABOUT 30.

WINNIE ODELL

SARA'S RUGELACH

1 cup butter
1 package (1 scant table-
    spoon) dry yeast
3 egg yolks

2 tablespoons sugar
3 cups flour
1 cup light cream

Sugar mixture:
1 cup sugar
2 tablespoons cinnamon

1 cup chopped walnuts

Wash:
1 egg white, beaten

Melt butter; let cool to about 100°F and add yeast. Stir to dissolve. Add egg yolks beaten with 2 tablespoons sugar. Alternate adding flour and cream to butter mixture. Mix well. Refrigerate overnight in mixing bowl. The next day, mix together sugar, cinnamon, and walnuts. Shape dough into a ball and divide into four sections. Roll out one section at a time and sprinkle with one-quarter of sugar mixture. Cut dough into small triangles and roll up. Repeat with remaining sections of dough and topping. Brush rolls with beaten egg white. Bake at 375°F on lightly greased cookie sheets for about 25 minutes. MAKES ABOUT 4 DOZEN.

MICHELINA PRENCIPE: *"This lovely recipe was given to me by a lovely friend, Sara Rubington. It's been in her family for a long time."*

SPICY NUT RUGELACH

8 ounces cream cheese
1/2 cup butter
2 cups flour
3 tablespoons butter,
  melted

1 cup finely chopped
  walnuts
3 tablespoons sugar
1 teaspoon cinnamon

Mix cream cheese, butter, and flour together. Chill to firm dough. Roll out about one-third of the dough on a floured board in a circle. Brush with 1 tablespoon of the melted butter. Combine walnuts, sugar, and cinnamon and sprinkle one-third of the mixture over the dough. Cut into 12 long triangles, and roll up starting with the short end so that the point is on the outside. Repeat with rest of dough and sugar mixture. Place on ungreased cookie sheets and bake at 350°F for about 10 or 15 minutes, until lightly browned. Cool on rack. MAKES 36.

WINNIE ODELL: *"You can vary the filling by using apricot jam or tiny chocolate chips."*

HUSAREN PENNIES

2 1/4 cups flour
1 cup butter
1 cup hazelnuts, ground
   fine

1 cup sugar
Currant jelly

Mix flour, butter, hazelnuts, and sugar in a bowl. Using your hands, knead all ingredients together, form dough into a ball, and place in refrigerator, covered, to firm. Roll small pieces into 1" balls. Place balls on a lightly greased cookie sheet and make a deep thumbprint in the center of each. Bake at 375°F until golden. Cool on racks. Liquefy the jelly in a double boiler over simmering water. Fill the thumbprints with the jelly and let cool. MAKES ABOUT 36.

HANNELORE HANCOCK

ANISPLÄTZCHEN
(ANISE COOKIES)

3 eggs
1 cup plus 2 tablespoons
  sugar
1 3/4 cups flour
1/2 teaspoon baking powder

1/2 teaspoon salt
1 1/2 teaspoons anise extract

In a large bowl, with electric mixer at medium speed, beat eggs until fluffy. Gradually beat in sugar. Continue beating for *20 minutes longer.* At lowest speed, beat in flour, baking powder, and salt; beat for one minute. Add anise extract and beat just until blended. Drop by teaspoonfuls, 1/2" apart, onto greased and floured cookie sheets. Swirl each spoonful to make a circular design. Let stand at room temperature, uncovered, for 8 hours or overnight. Preheat oven to 325°F. Bake cookies for about 10 minutes, until smooth and firm when pressed with fingertip. Cool on wire rack. Store in an airtight container. MAKES 5 DOZEN.

LAUREL GABEL

ZIMTSTERNE
(CINNAMON STARS)

1 pound shelled almonds,
blanched or unblanched
4 egg whites
1/4 teaspoon salt
3 cups confectioners'
sugar, sifted before measuring

1 tablespoon lemon juice
1 1/2 tablespoons cinnamon

In a food processor, grind the almonds until fine. Beat the egg whites with a mixer until soft peaks form. Add salt, and gradually beat in the sugar. Set aside 1/2 cup of this mixture for a glaze. Stir the almonds, lemon juice, and cinnamon into the remaining egg-white mixture and let stand for an hour to soften the almonds. Refrigerate or freeze to make dough easier to handle. Roll out small portions of the mixture to 1/4" thick on a board sprinkled with confectioners' sugar. Cut into star shapes. Let stand at room temperature for 3 to 4 hours. Spread reserved egg-white-mixture glaze on top of each cookie. Bake at 300°F for 25 minutes, or at 275°F for 30 minutes. Glaze should remain light in color. Cool on wire racks and store in an airtight container. MAKES ABOUT 4 DOZEN.

MIMI SAMOUR

MANDEL (ALMOND) BREAD

1/2 cup vegetable shortening or margarine
1 cup sugar
2 eggs, well beaten
2 teaspoons vanilla
1/2 teaspoon lemon juice
2 1/2 cups flour
2 teaspoons baking powder
1/2 teaspoon baking soda
1/4 teaspoon salt
1/2 cup candied cherries
1/2 cup raisins
1/2 cup almonds
Cinnamon and sugar for topping

Cream shortening and sugar. Add eggs, vanilla, and lemon juice. Sift dry ingredients together and add to creamed mixture. Cut up cherries and add to mixture along with raisins and almonds. Wet hands and shape dough on greased cookie sheet into 4 strips. Sprinkle with cinnamon and sugar. Place on top rack of oven. Bake at 375°F for 20 to 25 minutes. (Do not bake too long or bread will dry out.) Slice while still warm.

CEIL FISHMAN *(Mrs. Fishman, now deceased, brought this bread to the Cookie Exchange many times.)*

NUT BISCUITS

1 cup sugar
3 eggs
1/3 cup oil
1/4 cup water
3 cups flour
2 teaspoons baking
  powder
2 teaspoons cinnamon

1 teaspoon ground cloves
3/4 cup almonds, chopped
  or sliced
3/4 cup filbert nuts,
  chopped or sliced
Rind of one orange, grated
1 tablespoon sugar

Beat 2 of the eggs and add sugar and oil, beating to blend well. Add water. Sift together flour, baking powder, cinnamon, and cloves. Mix into creamed mixture. Stir in nuts and orange rind and blend well. Divide dough into 6 parts. Roll each part on a floured board and shape into a loaf. Press each loaf a little. Place the loaves on a large cookie sheet. Beat the remaining egg and brush it on top of the loaves. Sprinkle with sugar. Bake in a 350°F oven for 25 minutes until lightly browned. Remove loaves and cool slightly. Cut each loaf diagonally into biscuits. MAKES 5 TO 6 DOZEN BISCOTTI.

LUCY CORTICELLI

ZIA PAOLINA'S BUSCETTINI

4 cups sifted flour
3 cups toasted almonds,
  ground in blender
1 cup butter, melted
1/4 teaspoon salt
3 eggs, beaten

1 cup sugar
1 teaspoon vanilla
White wine (about 1/2
  cup)
1 egg, beaten, for wash

Place flour and ground almonds in a large bowl. Make a well in the center. Add melted butter and salt, and mix well. Add 3 beaten eggs, sugar, and vanilla. Mix. Add wine slowly to make a dough that is neither too soft nor too dry. Turn dough out onto floured board. Divide into 4 portions. Pat each portion into a loaf shape and place on greased cookie sheets. Slash diagonally. Brush tops with beaten egg. Bake for about 20 minutes at 300°F. Cool on rack, then slice. MAKES ABOUT 48 PIECES.

MICHELINA PRENCIPE: *"This is my Aunt Pauline's recipe. She is 94 years old, still going strong, and is the boss of her kitchen. Most of the time she doesn't use measurements. This is how she dictated the recipe to me."*

JUNE'S BISCOTTI

2 cups flour
1/2 cup sugar
1/2 teaspoon baking
  powder
6 tablespoons butter

4 medium eggs, beaten
1/2 cup filberts, broken in
  half
1/2 cup almonds, broken
  in half
1 egg, beaten

Sift together flour, sugar, and baking powder into a bowl. Cut in butter. Add 4 beaten eggs, then add nuts. Grease a cookie sheet and spread the batter into 2 rectangular shapes, about 1/2" thick. Brush tops with beaten egg. Bake at 350°F for about 45 minutes, or until tops are brown. Cut into biscotti (3/4" slices) and turn each slice on its side on the cookie sheet. Turn oven down to 325°F and return cookie sheet to oven to let slices toast for about 10 minutes. Turn biscotti over and toast the other side, watching closely so they don't get too brown. MAKES 30 TO 40 BISCOTTI, DEPENDING ON THICKNESS.

MICHELINA PRENCIPE: *"This recipe was given to me by June Palatini of Lodi, New Jersey. It's a specialty for Christmas."*

ITALIAN CHOCOLATE COOKIES

3 eggs
1 1/3 cups sugar
2/3 cup vegetable oil
6 ounces chocolate chips,
　melted
1/2 cup cold, strong coffee
Grated rind of 1 lemon
Grated rind of 1 orange

4 1/2 cups flour
2 tablespoons cocoa
1 tablespoon baking
　powder
1 tablespoon cinnamon
Pinch of salt
1 cup toasted almonds or
　walnuts, chopped

Frosting:
3/4 pound confectioners'
　sugar
3 tablespoons cocoa
2 tablespoons vanilla

2 tablespoons soft butter
1/4 cup milk (approxi-
　mately)

Beat eggs, sugar, and oil together. Add chocolate, coffee, and lemon and orange rinds. Stir in dry ingredients and nuts. Chill dough until firm, for several hours or overnight. Shape into balls the size of a walnut and bake on greased cookie sheets at 325°F for about 15 minutes. Cool, then frost.

To make frosting: Stir confectioners' sugar and cocoa together; add vanilla and butter and mix well. Add 1/4 cup milk, more if needed to reach spreading consistency, and beat until smooth. MAKES ABOUT 75.

CHRIS COPPOLINO

PIZZELLE

6 extra-large eggs
1 1/4 cups sugar
1 cup butter or margarine,
  melted and cooled
6 tablespoons vanilla (this
  is correct)

3 1/2 cups flour
4 teaspoons baking
  powder

Preheat pizzelle iron for 10 to 15 minutes while preparing batter. Beat eggs until frothy. Gradually add sugar while continuing to beat. Beat until sugar is dissolved and batter is smooth. Add melted butter and vanilla. Sift flour with baking powder and add to egg mixture. Mix until smooth. Batter will be thick and sticky. Drop a heaping tablespoon of batter in center of the preheated pizzelle iron and bake until lightly browned. Repeat. Discard first and second pizzelles. MAKES ABOUT 40.

MARY BEVILACQUA

FRAPPE

3 eggs
3 tablespoons sugar
3 tablespoons butter,
  melted
3 tablespoons olive oil
1 teaspoon vanilla

1 teaspoon almond extract
Grated rind of 1 lemon
3 cups flour
1/2 teaspoon salt
Confectioners' sugar

Beat eggs and sugar. Add melted butter, oil, vanilla, almond extract, and lemon rind. Add flour and salt and knead well. Roll out as thin as possible, or use a pasta machine. Cut into 1" x 3" strips. Deep-fry in very hot melted vegetable shortening until crisp and golden. Sprinkle with confectioners' sugar. MAKES 4 TO 5 DOZEN.

LUCY CORTICELLI

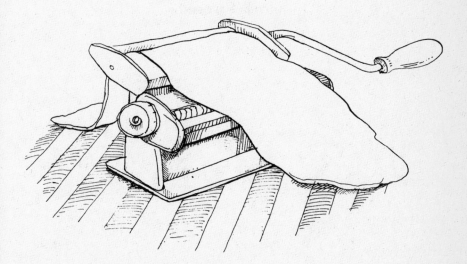

ANISEED BISCUITS

1/4 cup butter
1/2 cup sugar
2 eggs
2 cups flour
1 1/4 teaspoons baking
powder

1/4 teaspoon baking soda
1/4 teaspoon salt
1 teaspoon anise extract
1 1/2 teaspoons aniseed

Cream butter and sugar. Add eggs. Add flour, baking powder, baking soda, and salt, and mix well. Add anise extract and aniseed and blend. Shape with floured hands into 2 loaves 12″ to 15″ long and place on greased cookie sheet. Bake at 350°F for about 10 minutes, until light brown. Cool and frost with a mixture of 1 1/2 cups confectioners' sugar, 1 teaspoon vanilla, and enough milk to reach spreading consistency. Slice on the diagonal into 3/4″ pieces. MAKES ABOUT 30 SLICES.

CHRIS COPPOLINO

TOPFEN TRIANGLES

8 ounces cream cheese
8 ounces farmer's cheese
  (or cottage cheese that
  has been drained)
3/4 cup sugar
Grated rind of 1 lemon

1 egg yolk
1/2 cup golden raisins,
  soaked in dark rum
1 cup sweet butter
1 pound (about 24 sheets)
  strudel or phyllo dough

Place the cream cheese and farmer's cheese in a bowl. Mix together. Add sugar, lemon rind, egg yolk, and drained raisins. Melt the butter. Unroll the strudel dough. The thin sheets dry out rapidly, so be sure to keep them covered with a damp towel. Place one sheet on a floured board and brush it well with melted butter. Put a second sheet on top and brush with butter again. Cut sheets lengthwise into three equal strips. Place a teaspoonful of cheese filling at one end of each strip and fold up, flag style, to make triangles. Brush finished triangles with butter and place on buttered cookie sheets. Repeat with remaining strudel dough until strudel and filling are used up. Bake at 350°F for about 20 minutes. Cool on racks. MAKES 3 DOZEN.

MONICA FORMAN: *"I adapted this recipe from an Austrian strudel recipe. It's a labor of love—well worth the work."*

AUSTRIAN
FRIENDS' DELIGHT

3 eggs, separated
3/4 cup sugar
2 cups flour
1 cup blanched, slivered
  almonds

1 cup golden raisins,
  soaked in dark rum

Beat egg whites until stiff, then add sugar. Gently fold beaten egg yolks, flour, almonds, and drained raisins into the mixture and pour into a greased loaf pan. Bake at 325°F for about 35 minutes. Cool. Cut into thin slices and dry in a cool oven.

MONICA FORMAN

OLD WORLD
VIENNESE CRESCENTS

Vanilla sugar:

1/4 whole vanilla bean

1 cup sifted confectioners' sugar

Dough:

1 cup walnuts
1/4 teaspoon vanilla
1 cup butter

3/4 cup sugar
2 1/4 to 2 1/2 cups sifted flour

Make vanilla sugar by chopping the vanilla bean, then pulverizing it in a mortar and pestle or electric blender with 1 tablespoon of the confectioners' sugar. Mix thoroughly with rest of confectioners' sugar and set aside in a covered container, preferably overnight.

Mince the walnuts, then pound or process them to a paste. Using a wooden spoon or your fingers, mix the walnut paste, vanilla, butter, sugar, and flour to a smooth dough. Chill. Shape teaspoonfuls of dough into crescent shapes about 1 1/2″ long. Bake on ungreased cookie sheets until golden, about 15 to 18 minutes at 350°F. Cool briefly, then dust heavily with the prepared vanilla sugar. MAKES ABOUT 6 DOZEN.

LAUREL GABEL

LINZER SQUARES

2 cups flour
1 cup sugar
1/4 cup cocoa
1/2 teaspoon cinnamon
1/4 teaspoon nutmeg
1/4 teaspoon ground
  cloves
1/4 teaspoon ground
  ginger
1 egg

1/2 teaspoon vanilla (or to
  taste)
1/2 teaspoon almond ex-
  tract (or to taste)
1 cup unsalted butter or
  margarine
10 ounces seedless
  raspberry jam
Confectioners' sugar, for
  dusting

In food processor, place all dry ingredients and pulse until well mixed. Add egg, vanilla, and almond extract. Cut up butter into small pieces and add to mixture. Pulse until dough is well blended. (You can prepare the dough by hand by sifting together flour, sugar, cocoa, and spices. Then add egg, vanilla, and almond extract. Cut butter into small pieces and work into flour mixture with pastry blender or two knives until well blended.)

Knead dough briefly on a floured board, then form into a ball, wrap in waxed paper, and let rest for 1/2 hour. Cut dough in half. Roll out one half to fit a 9" x 9" square pan or a 10" round pan. Place in pan, pushing dough up sides a bit. Top with raspberry jam. Roll out second half of dough and cut into lattice strips. Crisscross them diagonally over the jam. Bake for about 40 minutes at 350°F. Run knife around edge, cut into squares, and dust with confectioners' sugar when cool. MAKES 16 TO 24, DEPENDING ON SIZE.

MONICA FORMAN: *"This is an old Austrian recipe."*

PRAGUE COOKIES

1/2 cup unsalted butter
3 tablespoons sugar

3 egg yolks
3/4 cup flour

Topping:
Apricot jam
3 egg whites

3/4 cup sugar
Cinnamon

Cream butter. Add sugar, yolks, and flour. Mix well. Spread in a buttered 9″ x 9″ pan. Cover with a thin layer of apricot jam. Beat egg whites until stiff, and add sugar gradually to make a meringue. Spread over jam layer and sprinkle lightly with cinnamon. Bake at 325°F until lightly browned (about 30 minutes). Cut into squares while still warm. MAKES ABOUT 36 SQUARES.

MONICA FORMAN: *"This is an old family recipe."*

PFEFFERNÜSSE

1 cup unblanched al-
monds
2 cups flour
1 teaspoon baking soda
1/4 cup dark corn syrup
1/2 cup butter
1/2 cup sugar
1 1/2 teaspoons cinnamon
1/2 teaspoon nutmeg
1/4 teaspoon ground
cloves
1/4 teaspoon black pepper
1/4 teaspoon salt
1 1/2 teaspoons grated
lemon rind
1 egg yolk
2 tablespoons heavy
cream
Confectioners' sugar

Coarsely grind the almonds. Mix them with flour and baking soda. In a saucepan, combine corn syrup, butter, sugar, cinnamon, nutmeg, cloves, black pepper, salt, and lemon rind. Heat, stirring, until butter melts. Cool slightly and beat in egg yolk and heavy cream. Beat in almond mixture gradually. Chill dough for 2 hours. Shape into 1" balls. Bake on ungreased cookie sheets at 375°F for 15 to 20 minutes, until the bottoms of the cookies are golden. Shake warm cookies a few at a time in a bag filled with confectioners' sugar. Store in covered containers for several days so flavors can develop. Recoat with sugar if desired before serving. MAKES 50 TO 60.

MIMI SAMOUR

LEBKUCHEN

1 egg
3/4 cup brown sugar, firmly packed
1/2 cup honey
1/2 cup dark molasses
3 cups flour
1 1/4 teaspoons nutmeg
1 1/4 teaspoons cinnamon

1/2 teaspoon baking soda
1/2 teaspoon ground cloves
1/2 teaspoon allspice
1/2 cup slivered almonds
1/2 cup mixed candied fruit and peels, finely diced

Beat egg. Add sugar, and beat until fluffy. Stir in honey and molasses. Sift together flour, nutmeg, cinnamon, baking soda, cloves, and allspice and add to first mixture. Beat well. Stir in nuts and fruit. Chill dough for several hours. On a floured surface, roll to 1/4" thick. Cut into squares or diamonds. Bake on greased cookie sheets at 350°F for about 10 to 12 minutes. Cool slightly and remove to racks to cool. While still warm, brush with lemon glaze (see recipe below). Add color after glazing by sprinkling cookies with colored sugar or small pieces of diced candied cherry. MAKES 3 TO 4 DOZEN, DEPENDING ON SIZE.

Lemon Glaze: Combine 1 slightly beaten egg white, 1 tablespoon lemon juice, 1/2 teaspoon grated lemon peel, dash of salt, and 1 1/2 cups confectioners' sugar. Mix well.

ELEANOR HOMEYER: *"These cookies need time to ripen before they are ready to eat. The German baker prepares them right after Thanksgiving to have them ready for Christmas. They are very satisfying to share with a friend who drops in for coffee."*

LEBKUCHEN II

1 pound strained honey
2 cups light brown sugar,
  firmly packed
1/4 cup water
1/2 teaspoon baking soda
8 cups flour
2 teaspoons cinnamon
1 teaspoon ground cloves

1 teaspoon nutmeg
2 eggs
1/2 pound blanched,
  slivered almonds
1/4 pound mixed citron,
  candied orange peel, and
  candied lemon peel,
  finely diced

Put the honey, sugar, and water into a saucepan and boil for 5 minutes. Set aside to cool. Sift together the baking soda, flour, cinnamon, cloves, and nutmeg. In a large bowl, combine the honey mixture with the flour mixture, adding the flour gradually. Add the eggs one at a time and beat well. Add the almonds and fruit. Pat the dough into a loaf shape, wrap in plastic or waxed paper, and chill overnight. The next day, cut off pieces of the dough, roll thin, and cut into square, round, or oblong shapes. Bake on greased cookie sheets at 350°F until light brown, about 10 minutes. Make a glaze of confectioners' sugar and water and ice the cookies. A few drops of vanilla or lemon extract may be added to the glaze. Other traditional decorations: crushed barley sugar; crushed nut meats; colored sugar (to form the initials of friends).

Some of the dough can be used the night it is made: roll small pieces into balls, press a raisin or nutmeat into each ball, and bake at 350°F for about 10 minutes. These are called *Pflastersteine*, or cobblestones. Serve them warm from the oven with sweet cider. MAKES ABOUT 100.

When Yankee *magazine published its article about the Wellesley Cookie Exchange in 1982,* MRS. E. A. FLEISCHMANN *sent this recipe, accompanied by a note: "This is a thank-you to* MRS. ELEANOR HOMEYER *for sharing her recipes with us. It's been in the family for years. These are hard cookies that are made in our family traditionally the day after Thanksgiving. They will soften by Christmas if stored in airtight boxes."*

LEBKUCHEN III

4 eggs
1 pound brown sugar
2 cups flour, or enough to make a moist dough
2 teaspoons cinnamon
1 ounce aniseed

2 ounces finely chopped citron
2 ounces finely chopped orange rind
1/4 pound blanched almonds, finely chopped

Beat eggs and sugar. Mix in flour, cinnamon, aniseed, fruit, and almonds. Divide batter between two buttered 9" x 13" pans and bake for 30 minutes at 300°F. Cut into bars while warm. Ice with a mixture of 1 cup confectioners' sugar, 2 tablespoons water, and 1/2 teaspoon vanilla or rose water flavoring. MAKES ABOUT 60, DEPENDING ON SIZE.

MAUREEN ZOCK: *"I got this recipe from Kate Alden Hough in 1970. I have used it at Christmas time ever since."*

GERMAN SPICE COOKIES

4 1/2 cups flour
2 1/2 teaspoons baking
  powder
2 1/2 teaspoons cinnamon
1 teaspoon coriander
1/2 teaspoon each allspice,
  ground cloves, freshly
  grated nutmeg, and cardamom

1 cup sugar
1 cup butter
3 eggs
1 teaspoon vanilla
2 egg whites

Mix flour, baking powder, and spices in a large bowl. Make a well in the center and pour in sugar. Cut butter into small chunks and place on top of sugar along with 3 eggs and vanilla. Knead ingredients in the bowl by hand until a smooth dough forms. Shape into a 4″ thick roll and refrigerate in airtight wrapping for at least several hours. Cut 1″ thick slices from dough and place side by side on a sheet of waxed paper. Cover with another sheet and roll out to 1/4″ thick. Remove top sheet of waxed paper and cut dough with cookie cutters. Reroll scraps. Place cookies on lightly greased cookie sheets and bake at 350°F for 15 minutes, until light brown. Meanwhile, beat egg whites until frothy. Brush hot cookies with egg white and bake for 1 minute longer, until whites look shiny and set. Cool on racks. Store in airtight containers. MAKES ABOUT 6 DOZEN.

SUSAN MAHNKE PEERY: *"These cookies taste best a week after being baked, when the flavors have mingled and mellowed."*

6. CHOCOLATE:
When Only That Special Taste Will Do

BEACON HILL COOKIES

◆━━━━━━━━━━━━━━━━━━━━━━━━━━━━━━━━━━━━━━━◆

1 cup (6 ounces) chocolate
  bits
2 egg whites
Dash of salt
1/2 cup sugar

1/2 teaspoon vanilla
1/2 teaspoon vinegar
3/4 cup walnuts, coarsely
  chopped

In double boiler, melt chocolate bits over simmering water. Beat egg whites with a dash of salt until foamy. Gradually add sugar, beating well until stiff peaks are formed. Beat in vanilla and vinegar. Fold in melted chocolate and walnuts. Drop onto greased cookie sheets. Bake for 10 minutes at 350°F. MAKES 36.

MAUREEN ZOCK: *"This recipe was given to me 25 years ago by my mother-in-law, Mrs. Matthias J. Zock of Wellesley Hills. It was given to her by a friend; I have passed it down to my four daughters, and they will to theirs."*

GEMMA'S CHOCOLATE COOKIES

1/2 cup vegetable shortening, melted
1 cup sugar
2 eggs
2 teaspoons vanilla
2 ounces unsweetened
   chocolate, melted

1/2 cup milk
2 cups plus 2 tablespoons
   flour
2 teaspoons baking
   powder
1 cup chopped walnuts
Confectioners' sugar

Beat vegetable shortening and sugar. Add eggs, vanilla, chocolate, and milk, and mix well. Add flour, baking powder, and walnuts. Mix well. Chill for about 1 hour. Shape teaspoonfuls into balls and roll in confectioners' sugar. Place on lightly greased cookie sheets, allowing room for cookies to spread. Bake at 350°F for about 15 minutes. Cool on racks. MAKES ABOUT 40.

LUCY CORTICELLI

CHOCOLATE ALMOND MACAROONS

4 egg whites
2/3 cup sugar
1 1/2 cups grated baking
   chocolate

2 1/2 cups ground,
   blanched almonds
1 teaspoon almond extract

Beat egg whites until stiff. Add sugar, then add chocolate and almonds. Stir in almond flavoring. Form into small round cookies and bake on greased cookie sheets for about 20 minutes at 350°F. The macaroons should be crisp on top and soft inside. MAKES 36.

MONICA FORMAN

BURIED CHERRY COOKIES

1/2 cup butter
1 cup sugar
1 egg
1 1/2 teaspoons vanilla
1 1/2 cups flour
1/2 cup unsweetened
  cocoa
1/4 teaspoon baking soda
1/4 teaspoon baking
  powder

1/4 teaspoon salt
1 10-ounce jar (about 48)
  maraschino cherries
6 ounces (1 cup) semi-
  sweet chocolate chips
1/2 cup Eagle Brand
  sweetened condensed
  milk

In large bowl, cream butter. Add sugar and beat until fluffy.
Add egg and vanilla and mix well. Combine flour, cocoa,
baking soda, baking powder, and salt, and gradually add
dry mixture to the butter mixture, beating well. Chill
dough if necessary for easy handling. Shape into 1" balls
and place about 2" apart on ungreased cookie sheets. Make
a deep thumbprint in the center of each ball. Drain the
cherries, reserving juice. Place a cherry in each thumbprint. In a small saucepan, combine the chocolate chips
and the condensed milk and stir over low heat until chocolate is melted. Stir in about 4 teaspoons reserved cherry
juice. Spoon 1 teaspoon of frosting over each cherry, covering it completely. Bake at 350°F for about 10 minutes,
until edges are firm. MAKES ABOUT 48.

MARY BEVILACQUA: *"These were made by Lynne Casal
for the 1984 Cookie Exchange. They are very chocolaty
and festive."*

BLACK BOTTOMS

8 ounces cream cheese
1 egg
1/3 cup sugar
1/8 teaspoon salt
1 cup chocolate chips
1 1/2 cups flour
1 cup sugar
1/4 cup cocoa

1/2 teaspoon salt
1 teaspoon baking soda
1 cup water
1/3 cup oil
1 teaspoon white vinegar
1 teaspoon vanilla
Sugar
Chopped almonds

Mix cream cheese and egg in bowl. Add 1/3 cup sugar and 1/8 teaspoon salt. Beat well. Stir in chocolate chips and set aside. Sift together flour, 1 cup sugar, cocoa, salt, and baking soda. Add water, oil, vinegar, and vanilla and beat until well blended. Fill greased or lined muffin cups 1/3 full with the flour-cocoa batter. Top each with a heaping teaspoonful of cheese mixture. Sprinkle with sugar and chopped almonds. Bake at 350°F for 30 to 35 minutes. MAKES 12.

MARY BEVILACQUA: *"These are elegant miniature chocolate cheesecakes."*

CHOCOLATE SNAZZERS

1 cup sugar
3/4 cup butter
1 egg
1/4 cup light corn syrup
2 ounces (1/3 cup) semi-
   sweet chocolate, melted

1 3/4 cups flour
2 teaspoons baking soda
1 teaspoon cinnamon
1/4 teaspoon salt
Sugar

Cream sugar and butter until light. Add egg. Stir in corn syrup and melted chocolate. In a small bowl, combine flour, baking soda, cinnamon, and salt, and add gradually to chocolate mixture. Shape into balls using 1 level tablespoon for each. Roll in sugar. Bake on ungreased cookie sheets at 350°F for 15 minutes. MAKES 36.

MARY BEVILACQUA

NUTTY CHOCOLATE
DROP COOKIES

1 1/2 cups semi-sweet
  chocolate chips
4 tablespoons butter
3/4 cup sugar
1 egg
1 1/2 teaspoons vanilla

1/2 cup flour
1/2 teaspoon salt
1/4 teaspoon baking
  powder
1/2 cup chopped walnuts

In double boiler over simmering water, or in heavy saucepan over very low heat, melt 1 cup of the chocolate chips. Let cool. Cream butter and sugar. Add egg and vanilla. Blend in melted chocolate. Combine flour, salt, and baking powder and add to creamed mixture, mixing well. Stir in walnuts and remaining 1/2 cup chocolate chips. Drop teaspoonfuls of dough 2" apart onto greased cookie sheets. Bake at 350°F for 8 to 10 minutes. MAKES ABOUT 30.

LAUREL GABEL

FUDGY FRUITCAKE DROPS

1/4 cup butter
1/2 cup sugar
1 egg
1/2 cup grape jelly
1 teaspoon vanilla
1 cup flour
1/4 cup unsweetened
  cocoa
2 teaspoons baking powder

2 cups chopped walnuts
1 1/2 cups (8 ounces)
  raisins
6 ounces (1 cup) semi-
  sweet chocolate chips
Confectioners' sugar
  (optional)

In large mixing bowl beat butter for 30 seconds. Add sugar and beat until fluffy. Add egg, grape jelly, and vanilla. Blend well. Combine flour, cocoa, and baking powder and stir this mixture into butter mixture. Stir in nuts, raisins, and chocolate chips. Drop by rounded teaspoonfuls onto greased and floured cookie sheets. Bake at 350°F for about 10 minutes, until just set. Cool for 1 minute on pan, then remove to wire racks. If desired, sift confectioners' sugar over cooled cookies. MAKES ABOUT 50.

ROSALEE OAKLEY

CHOCOLATE MINT STICKS

2 eggs, beaten
1/2 cup melted butter
2 squares unsweetened
  chocolate, melted

1 cup sugar
1/2 teaspoon vanilla
1/2 cup flour

Frosting:
2 tablespoons butter
1 cup sifted confectioners'
  sugar
1 tablespoon light cream
1/2 teaspoon peppermint
  flavoring or 1–2 table-
  spoons crème de
  menthe

1/2 square unsweetened
  chocolate, melted
1 1/2 tablespoons melted
  butter

Combine all ingredients except flour; beat well. Blend in flour. Pour into a greased and floured 9" square pan. Bake at 350°F for 25 minutes. Cool.

To prepare frosting: Mix butter, sugar, cream, and peppermint flavoring. Spread over cooled baked layer. When frosting is firm, mix melted chocolate and butter and drizzle over all.

Place in refrigerator until firm. Cut into small sticks or squares and put in small cupcake papers. MAKES ABOUT 4 1/2 DOZEN.

MARY BEVILACQUA

DOUBLE FUDGE BROWNIES

2/3 cup butter
1 1/2 cups sugar
1/4 cup water
2 teaspoons vanilla
12 ounces (2 cups) semi-
sweet chocolate chips

4 eggs
1 1/2 cups flour
1/2 teaspoon baking soda
1/2 teaspoon salt
1 cup chopped nuts

In a small saucepan, combine butter, sugar, and water. Bring just to a boil, then remove from heat and stir in vanilla and 1 cup of chocolate chips. Stir until mixture is smooth and chocolate is melted. Place in large bowl. Add eggs, one at a time, beating well after each addition. Combine flour, baking soda, and salt; gradually add to chocolate mixture. Stir in nuts. Add remaining cup of chocolate chips. Spread in a greased 9" x 13" pan and bake at 325°F for 45 to 50 minutes. Cool and cut into bars. MAKES ABOUT 3 DOZEN.

SUSAN MAHNKE PEERY

MARBLED BROWNIE DELIGHTS

4 ounces German sweet cooking chocolate
5 tablespoons butter
3 ounces cream cheese
1 cup sugar
3 eggs

1/2 cup plus 1 tablespoon flour
1/2 teaspoon vanilla
1/2 teaspoon baking powder
1/4 teaspoon salt

Melt chocolate and 3 tablespoons of the butter over very low heat or in a double boiler over simmering water. Stir, then cool. Cream 2 tablespoons of the butter with the cream cheese. Gradually add 1/4 cup of the sugar, beating until fluffy. Blend in 1 egg, 1 tablespoon flour, and vanilla. Set aside. In a second bowl, beat 2 eggs until pale colored. Slowly add remaining 3/4 cup sugar. Beat until thickened. Add baking powder and 1/2 cup flour. Add melted chocolate. Put half of chocolate batter into greased 9" x 9" pan. Top with cheese mixture. Spoon remaining chocolate batter over top. Swirl a knife through all three layers to marbleize. Bake at 350°F for 35 minutes. MAKES 16 LARGE BROWNIES.

MARY BEVILACQUA: *"This recipe is from an old* Boston Globe *'Chat' column."*

PAIGE'S BROWNIES

1 cup butter
4 ounces unsweetened
  chocolate
4 eggs
2 cups sugar
2 teaspoons vanilla

1 1/2 cups flour
1 teaspoon baking powder
1/2 teaspoon salt
1/2 cup chopped walnuts
1/2 cup chocolate chips

Melt butter and chocolate over low heat. Set aside to cool. Beat eggs until light in color. Add sugar and vanilla and blend well. Stir in chocolate mixture. Add flour, baking powder, and salt, and mix well. Fold in nuts and chocolate chips. Bake in a greased 9" x 13" pan at 350°F for about 35 minutes. Cut into bars. MAKES ABOUT 36.

SUSAN MAHNKE PEERY

7. BARS AND SQUARES:

Cookies, Plain and Fancy,
Baked in a Pan

OATMEAL CHOCOLATE BARS

Filling:

2 tablespoons butter or margarine

6 ounces chocolate chips

1 can (5 1/3 ounces) evaporated milk

1/4 cup sugar

1/2 cup chopped nuts

Cookie base:

1/2 cup butter or margarine

1 cup brown sugar, firmly packed

1 egg

1 teaspoon vanilla

1 1/4 cups flour

1/2 teaspoon baking soda

2 cups quick oats

To prepare filling: In a heavy saucepan combine butter, chocolate chips, evaporated milk, and sugar. Bring to a rolling boil, stirring constantly. Remove from heat. Stir in nuts and cool.

To prepare base: Cream butter and sugar. Add egg and vanilla and beat until light and fluffy. Stir in flour, soda, and 1 3/4 cups of the oats until well blended. Press 2/3 of this mixture into the bottom of a buttered 9"-square pan. Spread with cooled chocolate filling. Mix remaining 1/4 cup oats with remainder of cookie base and crumble over filling. Bake at 350°F for 25 to 30 minutes. MAKES 36.

MARY ANN GROME

CHOCOLATE MARSHMALLOW SQUARES

1/2 cup butter
1 1/2 cups sugar
2 cups sifted flour
Pinch of salt
4 ounces unsweetened
chocolate
1 1/4 cups boiling water

3 eggs, beaten
2 teaspoons baking
powder
2 teaspoons vanilla
1 8-ounce jar
marshmallow Fluff

Icing:

1 1/2 cups confectioners'
sugar
2 ounces unsweetened
chocolate, melted
1 tablespoon butter

Pinch of salt
1 egg
1 teaspoon vanilla
2 to 4 tablespoons milk

Cream butter and sugar. Add flour and salt and mix well. Chop chocolate into small pieces and pour boiling water over them, stirring until chocolate melts. Add chocolate mixture to butter-flour mixture and refrigerate for at least 3 hours. Remove from refrigerator and blend in eggs, baking powder, and vanilla. Pour into greased 9" x 12" pan and bake at 350°F for 20 minutes. Remove from oven and immediately spread with marshmallow Fluff. Return to oven for 8 to 10 minutes, until set. Let cool on rack.

Meanwhile, prepare icing by combining all ingredients and blending well. Add enough milk to reach spreading consistency. Spread icing over squares and let set before cutting into bars. MAKES 36.

STEVE ZAKON: *"This recipe is dedicated to the memory of my Aunt Beatrice Kopel, who kept this recipe a well-guarded secret."*

CONGO BARS

2 3/4 cups flour
2 1/2 teaspoons baking
 powder
1/2 teaspoon salt
3 eggs

2 cups brown sugar,
 firmly packed
1 teaspoon vanilla
2/3 cup vegetable oil
6 ounces chocolate bits

Sift together flour, baking powder, and salt. In a separate bowl, beat eggs. Add sugar, vanilla, and oil. Stir in dry ingredients, then add chocolate bits. Spread on a greased jelly-roll pan and bake for 15 to 20 minutes at 350°F. Cool slightly before cutting. MAKES AT LEAST 36.

SUSAN BURR: *"This easy bar tastes similar to Toll House cookies."*

VIENNA CHOCOLATE BARS

1 cup butter or margarine
2 egg yolks
1/2 cup sugar
2 1/2 cups flour
1 10-ounce jar raspberry or
  apricot jam
1 cup semi-sweet chocolate bits

4 egg whites
1/4 teaspoon salt
1 cup sugar
2 cups finely chopped
  walnuts

Cream butter, egg yolks, and 1/2 cup sugar. Add flour, kneading with fingers to form a dough. Pat the dough into a greased 9" x 13" pan and bake for 15 to 20 minutes at 350°F. Remove from oven. Spread base with jam. Top with chocolate bits. Beat egg whites with salt until stiff. Fold in 1 cup sugar and 2 cups finely chopped walnuts. Gently spread on top of jam and chocolate bits. Bake for about 25 minutes at 350°F. Cut into 3" x 1" bars. MAKES ABOUT 30.

> LOUISE BOLLES: *"I was using a newspaper as a paint dropcloth when this recipe caught my eye. It sounded good, so I cut it out."*

MAGIC SEVEN-LAYER BARS

1/2 cup butter
1 1/2 cups graham cracker
crumbs
6 ounces (1 cup) semi-
sweet chocolate chips
1 cup shredded coconut

1 cup butterscotch chips
1 cup chopped walnuts
1 14-ounce can sweetened
condensed milk (not
evaporated milk)

Melt butter in a 9" x 13" pan. Sprinkle crumbs over butter and add remaining ingredients in layers as given. Bake at 350°F for about 30 minutes. MAKES ABOUT 40.

SUSAN MAHNKE PEERY: *"This recipe turns up nearly everywhere, it seems, but I first got it from my college friend, Chris Poplawski, in 1971. If you prefer a thicker bar, a 9" x 9" pan works fine. Bake for about 10 minutes longer."*

OH HENRY BARS

2/3 cup butter
1 cup brown sugar, firmly
  packed
1 tablespoon vanilla
1/2 cup light corn syrup

4 cups quick oats
6 ounces (1 cup) chocolate
  chips
2/3 cup chunky peanut
  butter

Cream butter and sugar. Add vanilla, corn syrup, and oats. Pat dough into lightly greased 9" x 13" pan. Bake at 350°F for 15 to 16 minutes (do not overbake). While dough is baking, melt chocolate chips and peanut butter together over low heat. Cool dough slightly, then spread chocolate mixture on top. Cool further, then cut into bars. MAKES ABOUT 40.

NANCY COPPOLINO: *"I clipped this recipe out of* The Boston Globe *'Chat' column years ago. They're as good as the candy bars, maybe better!"*

OATMEAL CARMELITAS

32 light caramels
5 tablespoons light cream
or evaporated milk
1 cup flour
1 cup quick rolled oats
3/4 cup brown sugar,
firmly packed

1/2 teaspoon baking soda
1/4 teaspoon salt
3/4 cup melted butter
1 cup (6 ounces) chocolate
chips
1/2 cup chopped pecans

Melt caramels in cream over simmering water in top of double boiler. Cool slightly. In a large mixing bowl, combine flour, oats, brown sugar, baking soda, salt, and melted butter. Press half of this mixture into the bottom of an 11" x 7" pan. Bake at 350°F for 10 minutes. Remove from oven. Sprinkle with chocolate chips and pecans. Spread carefully with caramel mixture. Sprinkle with remaining crumb mixture. Bake for an additional 15 to 20 minutes, until golden brown. Chill for at least one hour, then cut into bars. MAKES ABOUT 36.

ROSALEE OAKLEY

CHOCOLATE-DATE SQUARES

3/4 cup butter
1 cup (6 ounces) chocolate
chips
1 1/3 cups flour
1/4 cup sugar
1/2 teaspoon baking
powder
3/4 cup confectioners'
sugar
2 eggs

3/4 cup creamy peanut
butter
3/4 cup dates, minced or
ground
3/4 cup finely chopped
walnuts
2 tablespoons water
1 tablespoon vegetable
shortening

Melt 1/2 cup of the butter with 1/2 cup of the chocolate chips. Blend in flour and sugar and press mixture firmly into greased 9" x 13" pan. Bake at 350°F for 10 minutes. Meanwhile, combine baking powder and confectioners' sugar in mixing bowl; add eggs, remaining 1/4 cup butter, peanut butter, dates, walnuts, and water, and blend thoroughly. Let baked crust cool for 5 minutes, then spread date mixture over crust. Bake for 15 to 20 minutes, until golden. Cool. Melt remaining 1/2 cup chocolate chips with 1 tablespoon shortening over hot water in double boiler and spread over bars. If desired, sprinkle with additional chopped nuts. MAKES ABOUT 48.

MARGARET MAHNKE

GERTRUDE'S DATE-NUT BARS

1 cup flour
1/2 teaspoon baking
　powder
1/2 teaspoon salt
1/2 cup butter
1 cup sugar

2 eggs
1 teaspoon vanilla
One 6 1/2-ounce package
　chopped dates
1 cup chopped nuts
Confectioners' sugar

Combine flour, baking powder, and salt, and set aside.
Cream butter and sugar. Add eggs, beating well, then add
vanilla. Gradually add the dry ingredients. Stir in dates
and nuts. Pour into a greased 9″ x 9″ pan. Bake at 375°F
for about 30 minutes. Cool and sprinkle with confectioners' sugar. MAKES ABOUT 16 TO 20.

JACKIE FITZPATRICK

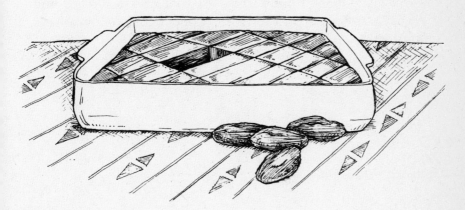

BUTTERMILK BARS

1 1/4 cups sugar
3/4 cup brown sugar,
  firmly packed
2 cups flour
1/2 cup butter, softened
1/2 cup shredded coconut
1/2 cup chopped nuts

1 egg, beaten
1/2 teaspoon salt
1 teaspoon cinnamon
1 teaspoon baking soda
1 cup buttermilk
1 teaspoon vanilla

Combine sugar, brown sugar, flour, and butter in a bowl and mix with a pastry blender until mixture is in coarse crumbs. Take out 2 cups of the mixture and reserve the rest. To the 2 cups add coconut and chopped nuts, and pat this mixture into a greased 9" x 13" pan. To the reserved mixture, add the egg, salt, cinnamon, baking soda, buttermilk, and vanilla, and mix well. Pour over the crumb mixture in the pan. Bake at 350°F for 45 minutes. Remove to rack and cool. Drizzle with a thin confectioners' sugar glaze made from 1 1/2 cups confectioners' sugar and enough milk or cream to reach proper consistency. MAKES ABOUT 48.

MARGARET MAHNKE

COCONUT-PECAN SQUARES

1/2 cup butter
1/2 cup dark brown sugar,
  firmly packed
1 cup flour
2 eggs
1 cup light brown sugar,
  firmly packed

1 cup chopped pecans
1/2 cup shredded coconut
  tossed with 2 table-
  spoons flour
1 teaspoon vanilla
Pinch of salt
Confectioners' sugar

Cream butter and dark brown sugar, then add 1 cup flour and mix well. Press into a greased 8" x 8" x 2" pan and bake at 350°F for 20 minutes. Meanwhile, beat the eggs until frothy. Gradually add light brown sugar and beat until thick. Add pecans, coconut tossed with flour, vanilla, and salt. Mix well. Spread over crust and bake an additional 20 minutes, until brown. Cool on rack. Sprinkle with confectioners' sugar and cut into 1" squares. MAKES ABOUT 36.

JEAN DE LONGCHAMP: *"Be sure to use dark and light brown sugars as directed."*

DREAM SQUARES

1/3 cup butter
1/4 cup sugar

1 egg
1 1/4 cups flour

Topping:

3 eggs
1 cup brown sugar, firmly
  packed
1/3 cup flour
1 teaspoon baking powder

Pinch of salt
1 teaspoon vanilla
1 cup shredded coconut
1 cup chopped walnuts

Cream butter and sugar with electric mixer. Beat in egg. Stir in flour, mixing until a soft dough forms. Spread evenly into a greased 9" x 9" pan. Bake for 12 minutes at 375°F, until dough begins to firm up but is not fully baked. Remove pan to wire rack and lower oven temperature to 350°F.

To make topping: Beat the 3 eggs and add brown sugar. Mix well. Add 1/3 cup of flour mixed with baking powder and salt. Add vanilla, coconut, and nuts. Mix well. Pour over baked base, and return to oven to bake for 35 to 40 minutes, until center is no longer fluid. Frost if desired with a mixture of 1 1/2 cups confectioners' sugar, 1 teaspoon almond extract, and enough cream or milk to reach spreading consistency. Cut into small bars. MAKES ABOUT 36.

ROSALEE OAKLEY: *"No refreshment table was complete at Central Congregational Church in Jamaica Plain, Massachusetts, in the early 1960s without Mrs. Isabella Ruddell's Dream Squares. They were (and are) delicious!"*

CRUNCHIES

2 cups oatmeal
1 cup flour
1 cup shredded coconut
Pinch of salt
7 ounces (1 3/4 sticks)
  butter

2/3 cup brown sugar,
  firmly packed
2 tablespoons honey
1 teaspoon baking soda

Mix oatmeal, flour, coconut, and salt together in a medium-size bowl. Melt butter and add brown sugar and honey. Add baking soda to butter mixture and add this mixture to the dry ingredients. Pour into a 9" x 13" baking pan. Bake at 275°F for 50 minutes. Cut into squares when cool. Store in an airtight container. MAKES ABOUT 40.

SUSAN MAHNKE PEERY: *"A note with this recipe, found on the back of a newspaper clipping, guesses that it is of English origin."*

SNIP DOODLES

2 tablespoons unsalted
  butter or shortening
1 cup sugar
4 eggs, separated
1/4 cup milk
2 teaspoons vanilla

1 cup flour
1 teaspoon baking powder
Butter
Sugar
Cinnamon

Cream butter and add sugar until mixture is creamy. Add egg yolks, milk, and vanilla, and mix well. Add flour and baking powder. Beat egg whites until soft and fold into mixture. Spread into well-greased 9″ round or square pan and bake at 375°F for 15 to 20 minutes. Immediately after removing from oven, top off with dabs of butter and sprinkle with a mixture of sugar and cinnamon. Cut into 1″ x 3″ strips to serve. MAKES ABOUT 24.

MONICA FORMAN: *"This is my mother's recipe. She always served snip doodles warm."*

NUTMEG FLATS

1 cup butter
1 cup sugar
1 egg, separated

2 cups flour
1 1/2 teaspoons freshly
  grated nutmeg

Cream butter and sugar. Add egg yolk. Add flour and nutmeg. Spread in a greased jelly-roll pan. Beat egg white lightly and spread over top of dough. Bake at 275°F for 55 to 65 minutes. Cut into 2″ x 2″ bars while still warm. MAKES ABOUT 36.

MAUREEN ROBINSON: *"These are simple to make and really delicious! The nutmeg flavor is very pronounced."*

MERINGUE BARS

3/4 cup butter or margarine
3/4 cup sugar
2 eggs, separated
1 1/2 cups sifted flour

1 cup apricot or raspberry preserves
1/2 cup coconut
1/2 cup sugar
1/2 cup walnuts, chopped

Beat butter and 3/4 cup sugar until well blended. Beat in egg yolks. Mix in flour, blending well. Mixture will be somewhat dry. Spread in a greased 9″ x 13″ pan and bake at 350°F for 15 minutes. Cool. Spread with preserves. Sprinkle with coconut. Beat egg whites until soft peaks form, then gradually beat in 1/2 cup sugar, beating until stiff. Fold in walnuts. Spread meringue over preserves and coconut. Bake at 350°F until light golden and slightly firm to the touch, about 20 to 25 minutes. Cool and cut into 1 1/2″ x 2″ bars. MAKES ABOUT 36.

Note: Instead of jam you could sprinkle the baked bottom layer with chocolate chips.

NANCY BURR

DATE-NUT MERINGUE BARS

8 ounces chopped dates
1/4 to 1/2 cup water
3/4 cup butter
3/4 cup sugar

2 eggs, separated
1 1/2 cups flour
1/2 cup sugar
1/2 cup chopped nuts

Combine dates and water and cook over medium heat to a soft, jamlike consistency. Set aside. Combine butter and 3/4 cup sugar, and beat until creamy. Beat in egg yolks. Mix in flour to make a thick batter. Spread in a greased 9" x 13" pan, or two 8" pans. Bake at 350°F for 15 minutes. Remove to rack, cool slightly, and spread with date mixture. Beat egg whites until soft peaks form, then gradually beat in 1/2 cup sugar, beating until stiff. Fold in chopped nuts. Spread meringue over date mixture. Return to oven and bake at 350°F until light golden, about 20 to 25 minutes. Cool and cut into bars. MAKES 24 LARGE BARS OR 48 SMALLER ONES.

NANCY PLATTS: *"I prefer to cut these bars into small pieces, because they are very rich."*

WALNUT CHEWS

1 egg
1 cup brown sugar, firmly
 packed
1 teaspoon vanilla
1/2 cup flour

1/4 teaspoon baking soda
1/4 teaspoon salt
1 cup coarsely chopped
 walnuts

Stir together egg, brown sugar, and vanilla. Quickly add flour, baking soda, and salt. Stir in walnuts. Spread in a greased 8″ x 8″ pan and bake at 350°F for 18 to 20 minutes. (Do not overbake. Dough will be soft in center when you remove it from the oven.) Cool in pan. Cut in 2″ squares. MAKES 16.

SUSAN MAHNKE PEERY

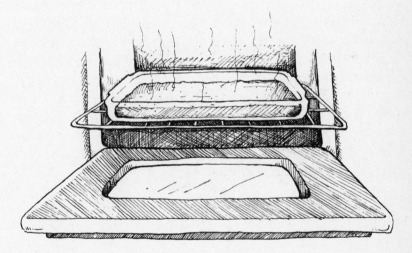

PECAN DIAMONDS

1/3 cup butter
1/4 cup sugar
1 egg
1 1/4 cups flour
1/2 cup butter
1/3 cup dark brown sugar,
  firmly packed

3 tablespoons sugar
1/3 cup honey
2 tablespoons heavy
  cream
6 ounces pecans, coarsely
  chopped (walnuts may
  be substituted)

Beat 1/3 cup butter with 1/4 cup sugar in a small bowl
with electric mixer until light and fluffy. Beat in egg. Stir
in flour, mixing well, until a soft dough forms. Spread
evenly into a lightly greased 9" x 9" pan. Bake at 375°F for
12 minutes, or until dough begins to firm up but is not
fully baked. Remove pan to wire rack and lower oven
temperature to 350°F. Meanwhile, melt remaining 1/2 cup
butter in a medium saucepan. Add brown sugar, the 3
tablespoons sugar, and honey. Bring to a boil and boil rapidly for 2 1/2 minutes. (The mixture will be caramel colored and thick.) Carefully add cream and return to a boil.
Remove from heat; stir in pecans. Spread mixture evenly
over cookie dough. Bake at 350°F for 25 minutes, or until
pecan mixture is bubbly and begins to set. Cool completely on wire rack (pecan topping will become firm).
Cut into 8 lengthwise strips and 9 diagonal strips. MAKES
80 DIAMOND-SHAPED COOKIES.

ROSALEE OAKLEY: *"The combination of shortbread cookie
topped with pecan toffee candy is irresistible!"*

GERMAN HONEY BARS

1 3/4 cups flour
1/2 cup sugar

2 teaspoons baking powder
1/2 cup butter

Honey topping:
1/3 cup sugar
1/4 cup honey
1/4 cup whipping cream

1/4 cup flour
1 cup sliced almonds

Place flour, sugar, baking powder, and butter in a mixing bowl and mix together until crumbly. Pat into a buttered 7" x 11" pan. Bake at 350°F for 10 minutes. Meanwhile, make the topping. Place sugar, honey, and cream in a saucepan and bring to a boil. Cook until the temperature reaches 190°F on a candy thermometer. Remove from the heat and whisk in flour. Stir in nuts. Spread on top of the crust and bake for 10 minutes longer. Cool on a rack, then cut into bars. MAKES ABOUT 4 1/2 DOZEN.

LOUISE BOLLES

BUTTERCRUNCH BARS

1 cup butter, melted
1 cup brown sugar, firmly
  packed
1 egg, separated
1 teaspoon vanilla

2 cups flour
Pinch of salt
1 cup finely chopped
  walnuts or pecans
1 cup chocolate chips

Combine melted butter and brown sugar and stir well. Add egg yolk and vanilla and blend. Stir in flour and salt. Dough will be very moist. Pat dough into greased 15" x 10" x 1" jelly-roll pan. Stir egg white with a fork and brush onto dough with pastry brush. Sprinkle with chopped nuts and chocolate chips, distributing them evenly. Bake at 375°F for about 20 minutes, until crust is golden brown. Cool and cut into bars. MAKES ABOUT 4 DOZEN.

SUSAN MAHNKE PEERY

TOFFEE SQUARES

1 cup butter
1 cup light brown sugar,
firmly packed
1 egg yolk
2 cups flour
1 teaspoon vanilla

Six 1.05-ounce milk chocolate bars, or 6 ounces semi-sweet chocolate chips
2/3 cup finely chopped nuts

Cream butter and sugar. Add egg yolk. Add flour and vanilla and stir until well blended. Spread dough into greased 15" x 10" x 1" jelly-roll pan and bake at 350°F for 15 to 20 minutes, until golden brown. Remove from oven and immediately lay chocolate bars or chips on top of crust. Allow chocolate to soften, and spread evenly. Sprinkle with chopped nuts, and press nuts lightly into chocolate, using the bottom of a glass. Cool, then cut into bars. MAKES AT LEAST 3 DOZEN, DEPENDING ON SIZE.

This recipe was submitted by Lucille Billings, Parky Waugh, Margaret Mahnke, and Janet Meany. It's popular!

MINNESOTA SQUARES
(GRAHAM NUT TOFFEE SQUARES)

12 whole (double) graham
crackers
1 cup butter

1 cup brown sugar, firmly
packed
1 1/2 cups chopped pecans

Lay crackers in jelly-roll pan so that bottom of pan is
completely covered. Melt the butter and sugar together,
bring to a boil, and cook for exactly 2 minutes. Pour syrup
over crackers. Sprinkle with nuts. Bake at 350°F for 8
minutes. Cool slightly before cutting. MAKES ABOUT 48.

LAUREL AND MARY

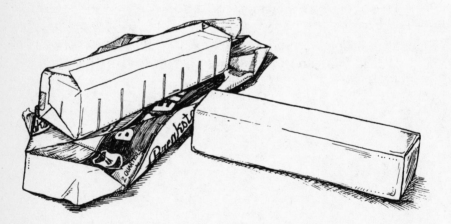

CHEESECAKE DREAMS

1/3 cup brown sugar,
firmly packed
1/2 cup chopped walnuts
1 cup flour
1/3 cup butter, melted
8 ounces cream cheese

1/4 cup sugar
1 egg
1 tablespoon lemon juice
2 tablespoons cream or
milk
1 teaspoon vanilla

Mix brown sugar, nuts, and flour together in a large bowl. Stir in the butter and mix with your hands until crumbly. Remove 1 cup of the mixture and reserve for topping. Press remainder firmly into an 8" square pan. Bake at 350°F for 12 to 15 minutes. Meanwhile, beat cream cheese until smooth and add sugar. Beat in the egg, lemon juice, cream, and vanilla. Pour onto the baked crust. Top with reserved crumbs. Return to oven and bake for about 25 minutes longer. Cool thoroughly, then cut into 2" squares. These can be baked the day before serving. Cover with plastic wrap and keep refrigerated. MAKES ABOUT 16 BARS.

MICHELINA PRENCIPE: *"I don't remember who gave this to me, but it's been a favorite for a long time."* Rosalee Oakley also sent in this recipe.

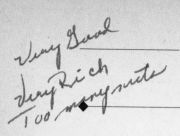
Very Good
Very Rich
Too many nuts

ALMOND CROSTATA

2 eggs
3/4 cup sugar
1/4 cup butter, melted
2 tablespoons vegetable
  shortening, melted

2 teaspoons rum or 1
  teaspoon rum extract
2 1/2 cups flour
2 teaspoons baking
  powder

Filling:

2 cups chopped, blanched,
  slivered almonds
1 cup chopped walnuts
2 eggs, beaten
2 teaspoons almond
  extract

5 tablespoons amaretto
  liqueur
5 tablespoons sugar
5 tablespoons chocolate,
  melted and cooled

Beat eggs and sugar. Add melted butter and melted vegetable shortening, rum, flour, and baking powder. Mix well, and roll out 2/3 of dough between 2 sheets of waxed paper to fit a 9" x 13" pan. Line pan with dough. Mix together filling ingredients and spread over dough. Roll out remaining dough and cut into strips; arrange them crisscross style over the filling. Bake at 350°F for 25 to 30 minutes, or until light brown. When crostata comes out of the oven, you may sprinkle it very lightly with drops of amaretto. Cut into slices. MAKES ABOUT 36.

LUCY CORTICELLI

ALMOND GENOISE

2 jumbo or 3 small eggs,
  beaten
3/4 cup sugar
1/2 cup corn oil
1 cup flour
1 1/2 teaspoons almond
  extract

Pinch of salt
1/2 teaspoon baking
  powder
Confectioners' sugar for
  sprinkling

Place beaten eggs in large bowl and add all remaining ingredients. Mix thoroughly. Pour into a greased 9″ square pan. Bake at 350°F for 20 minutes. Sprinkle with confectioners' sugar. When cool, cut into bars. MAKES ABOUT 30.

CHRIS COPPOLINO

APPLE STRIPS

3/4 cup unsalted butter (or half butter, half margarine)
2 cups flour
1/4 cup sugar
3 tablespoons sour cream

1/2 teaspoon grated lemon rind
Egg yolk for wash
Confectioners' sugar (optional)

Filling:

4–5 medium Macintosh apples, peeled and thinly sliced

1 tablespoon raisins
1/2 cup sugar

Work butter into flour with a fork and add sugar, sour cream, and lemon rind, kneading to form a dough. Form into a roll, wrap in waxed paper, and let rest for half an hour. Cut roll in half. Roll out one part to fit a 9" x 9" pan. Line with apple slices and sprinkle with raisins and sugar. Roll out remaining dough and cut into strips to form a lattice pattern on top of the apples. Brush with egg yolk to which a little cold water has been added. Bake at 325°F for about 20 minutes, until golden brown. Dust with confectioners' sugar while still warm, if desired, and cut into 1" x 2" strips. MAKES ABOUT 30.

MONICA FORMAN: *"These apple slices, made from an Austrian recipe, can be served warm or cold."*

APPLESAUCE-DATE BARS

3/4 cup butter
1 cup sugar
2 eggs
2 cups unsweetened apple-
　sauce
1 teaspoon vanilla
2 cups flour

1 teaspoon cinnamon
1/2 teaspoon ground
　cardamom
2 teaspoons baking soda
Pinch of salt
1 cup chopped dates
1 cup chopped walnuts

Cream butter and sugar. Add eggs and beat well. Add applesauce and vanilla. Combine flour, cinnamon, cardamom, baking soda, and salt, and add to butter mixture. Stir in dates and walnuts. Bake in a greased 9″ x 13″ pan at 350°F for about 30 minutes. Cool on a rack, then frost.

To make frosting: Combine 1/4 cup soft butter, 1 1/2 cups confectioners' sugar, 1/2 teaspoon vanilla, and enough boiling water to make a smooth frosting. Beat well, then stir in grated rind of one orange. MAKES 30.

SUSAN MAHNKE PEERY

APRICOT SQUARES

3/4 cup butter or marga-
rine
1 cup sugar
1 egg, beaten
1 teaspoon vanilla
1/2 teaspoon salt

2 cups flour
1 3/8 cups shredded
coconut
3/4 cup chopped nuts
1 jar (10 or 12 ounces)
apricot jam

Cream shortening and add sugar and beaten egg. Stir in vanilla and salt. Add flour, coconut, and nuts. Mix well. Spread 3/4 of dough in 7" x 11" pan. Press firmly with hand. Spread apricot jam over dough. Crumble remainder of dough over jam. Bake at 350°F for about 30 minutes. Allow to cool, then cut into squares. MAKES ABOUT 3 DOZEN.

ROSALEE OAKLEY AND JANET MEANY

DATE-NUT-APRICOT BARS

1/2 cup chopped dates
1/4 cup chopped dried
  apricots
1/4 cup raisins
1/3 cup dark rum
1/4 cup butter, melted
1 cup sugar

3 eggs, well beaten
1 cup flour
1/2 teaspoon baking
  powder
Dash of salt
1 cup chopped pecans
Confectioners' sugar

Three hours before baking, soak dates, apricots, and raisins in rum. Mix remaining ingredients except confectioners' sugar in the order given, adding the fruit-rum mixture last. Spread in a greased 9" x 13" pan and bake at 350°F until delicately brown (about 30 minutes). Cut in finger-shaped pieces and roll in confectioners' sugar while still warm. MAKES ABOUT 40.

MIMI SAMOUR

APRICOT OATMEAL BARS

Dough:

1 1/4 cups flour
1 1/4 cups rolled oats
1/2 cup sugar
3/4 cup butter, melted

1/2 teaspoon baking soda
1/4 teaspoon salt
2 teaspoons vanilla

Filling:

10 ounces apricot
   preserves

1/2 cup shredded coconut

In a large mixing bowl combine all dough ingredients and mix until crumbly. Reserve 1 cup of the mixture and press the remainder into a greased 9" x 13" pan. Spread the apricot preserves to within 1/2" of the edge of the crumb base; sprinkle with the reserved crumbs and the coconut. Bake at 350°F for about 25 minutes, until edges are lightly browned. MAKES AT LEAST 3 DOZEN.

> SUSAN MAHNKE PEERY: *"This recipe came from a promotional booklet put out by a butter company. You can vary the type of preserves; raspberry makes a delicious bar as well."*

BUTTER PECAN
BANANA BARS

2 1/2 cups flour
1 2/3 cups sugar
1 1/4 teaspoons baking
  powder
1 1/4 teaspoons baking
  soda
1/2 teaspoon salt

3/4 cup butter, softened
2/3 cup buttermilk
3 medium-size ripe
  bananas, mashed
2 eggs
1/2 cup chopped pecans

Combine flour, sugar, baking powder, baking soda, and salt in large mixing bowl. Add softened butter, cut in chunks, buttermilk, and bananas, and beat well using an electric mixer. Add eggs and mix well. Stir in nuts. Bake in an ungreased 15" x 10" x 1" pan for 30 to 35 minutes. Cool. Frost if desired with a mixture of 1/4 cup soft butter, 1 1/2 cups confectioners' sugar, 1/2 teaspoon vanilla, and enough milk to reach spreading consistency. Beat frosting ingredients until smooth, and fold in 1/2 cup finely chopped pecans. MAKES 48 BARS.

SUSAN MAHNKE PEERY

CHERRY MACAROONS

1 cup sifted flour
1/2 cup butter or
  margarine
3 tablespoons confection-
  ers' sugar
2 eggs, slightly beaten

1 cup sugar
1/4 cup flour
1 teaspoon vanilla
1/2 cup shredded coconut
1/2 cup coarsely chopped
  maraschino cherries

Combine 1 cup flour, butter, and confectioners' sugar. Mix well, and press into greased 8" x 8" pan. Bake at 350°F for 25 minutes. Meanwhile, combine eggs, sugar, 1/4 cup flour, vanilla, coconut, and cherries. Mix together and spread over top of baked crust. Return to oven and bake for 20 to 25 minutes longer. Cool and cut into squares. MAKES ABOUT 30.

CEIL FISHMAN

CRANBERRY SQUARES

4 eggs
2 cups sugar
2 cups flour
1/2 teaspoon salt
1/2 cup butter, melted

1 teaspoon orange extract
1 cup chopped walnuts
2 cups chopped cran-
  berries

Beat the eggs with a wire whip, then add sugar and beat well. Add flour and salt. Add butter, orange extract, walnuts, and cranberries, and mix well. Pour into a greased 9" x 9" pan, or in a 9" x 13" pan if you like a thinner bar.

Bake at 350°F for about 30 minutes. (Baking time will be shorter if you use a larger pan.) Cut into bars of desired size. MAKES 30 TO 45.

DORIS MORSE

FRUIT LAYER CAKES

◆━━━━━━━━━━━━━━━━━━━━━━━━━━━━━━━━━━━◆

1 1/2 cups sifted flour
1 tablespoon sugar
1/2 teaspoon salt
6 tablespoons butter
2 eggs, separated
1/4 cup sour cream
1/2 teaspoon vanilla
1 cup finely chopped dates

3/4 cup sour cream
1/3 cup apricot preserves
2 teaspoons grated orange rind
7 tablespoons sugar
1/2 teaspoon cinnamon
1/3 cup chopped walnuts

Combine flour, 1 tablespoon sugar, salt, and butter in a bowl and mix with pastry blender until mixture forms coarse crumbs. Stir in egg yolks, 1/4 cup sour cream, and vanilla. Pat this mixture into a greased 9″ x 13″ pan. Bake at 350°F for 20 minutes. Combine dates, 3/4 cup sour cream, apricot preserves, and orange rind. Spread this over baked layer. Beat the egg whites to soft peaks. Gradually add 7 tablespoons sugar and cinnamon. Beat until soft peaks form. Carefully spread meringue on top of date mixture. Sprinkle with chopped walnuts. Bake at 350°F for 30 minutes, or until browned. Cool and cut into 1 1/2″ squares. MAKES 4 DOZEN SQUARES.

LAUREL GABEL

LEMON SQUARES

2 cups flour
1/2 cup confectioners'
   sugar
1 cup butter or margarine,
   melted
4 eggs

2 cups sugar
1/3 cup lemon juice
1/2 teaspoon baking
   powder
1/4 cup flour

Mix together 2 cups flour, confectioners' sugar, and melted butter. Spread into a 9″ x 13″ pan and bake at 350°F for 25 minutes. Mix eggs, sugar, lemon juice, baking powder, and 1/4 cup flour and pour onto the baked shell. Bake at 350°F for an additional 25 minutes, or until set. Dust with confectioners' sugar when cool, if desired. Cut into bars of desired size. MAKES AT LEAST 36.

NANCY BURR: *"I obtained this recipe at a bridal shower when the squares were served as refreshments. They are delicious and easy to make—the two things I like best about cooking."*

LEMON BARS

1 cup butter
2 cups flour
1/2 cup confectioners'
  sugar
1/2 teaspoon salt

4 eggs, beaten
6 tablespoons lemon juice
1 1/2 cups sugar
4 tablespoons flour
1 teaspoon baking powder

Combine butter, 2 cups flour, confectioners' sugar, and salt with pastry blender, mixing until mixture is like streusel, or coarse crumbs. Reserve one cup of the mixture to use as topping, and press the remainder into a greased 9" x 13" pan. Bake for 20 minutes at 350°F. Meanwhile, mix the filling: combine eggs, lemon juice, sugar, 4 tablespoons flour, and baking powder, and mix well. Spread over baked crust and sprinkle with remaining cup of topping. Bake for 20 to 25 minutes longer at 350°F. Remove from oven and let cool. Sprinkle with confectioners' sugar and cut into bars. MAKES ABOUT 40.

MARGARET MAHNKE

LEMON LOVE NOTES

1/2 cup butter
1 cup sifted flour
1/4 cup confectioners'
  sugar
1 cup sugar
2 tablespoons flour

1/2 teaspoon baking
  powder
2 eggs, beaten
2 tablespoons lemon juice
2 teaspoons lemon rind

Mix butter, 1 cup flour, and confectioners' sugar and press mixture into an 8″ x 8″ pan. Bake at 350°F for 8 to 10 minutes. Cool. Combine sugar, 2 tablespoons flour, baking powder, eggs, lemon juice, and lemon rind, and mix well. Pour over crust. Bake for 25 minutes longer. Cool. Cut into squares and dust with confectioners' sugar. MAKES ABOUT 30.

> LAUREL GABEL: *"These squares cut more easily if you freeze them slightly first."*

MARMALADE BARS

1/2 cup butter
1 cup brown sugar, firmly
  packed
1 egg
2 tablespoons orange juice
1 cup rolled oats
1 1/2 cups flour

1 teaspoon baking powder
1/4 teaspoon baking soda
1/4 teaspoon salt
1 cup orange marmalade
1/2 cup chopped walnuts
1/2 cup shredded coconut

In mixing bowl, cream butter and gradually add brown sugar until mixture is light. Add egg and orange juice and beat well. Stir in oats. Combine flour, baking powder, baking soda, and salt, and add to butter mixture. Spread half of batter in a greased 9″ x 13″ pan. Combine marmalade, walnuts, and coconut in a small bowl and spread over batter in pan. Drop remaining batter by spoonfuls over filling, and spread carefully. Bake at 350°F for 30 to 35 minutes, until golden. If desired, frost while warm with a mixture of 2 tablespoons soft butter, 1 1/2 cups confectioners' sugar, 1 teaspoon grated orange rind, and enough orange juice to bring mixture to spreading consistency. Or cool and serve unfrosted with vanilla ice cream. MAKE ABOUT 40.

MARGARET MAHNKE: *"This recipe came from one of the Pillsbury Bake-Offs. You can make a chewier bar by using a 9″ square pan and reducing the marmalade to 3/4 cup."*

ORANGE SQUARES

1 whole seedless orange,
  unpeeled
1 cup raisins
1/3 cup butter or marga-
  rine
1 cup sugar
2 eggs

1 teaspoon baking soda
3/4 cup sour cream or
  plain yogurt
1 3/4 cups flour
Pinch of salt

Cut orange into quarters and grind with raisins, preferably using a heavy iron meat grinder with a coarse blade.
(A food processor will also do the job, but be sure not to
grind the fruit to mush.) Cream butter and sugar. Add
eggs. Add orange mixture and blend well. Dissolve the
baking soda in the sour cream or yogurt and add to orange
mixture. Add flour and salt, and stir by hand until well
mixed. Spread in a greased jelly-roll pan. Bake at 350°F
for 20 to 30 minutes. Cool. Dust with confectioners' sugar,
or make an orange-flavored confectioners'-sugar icing by
combining 1 1/2 cups confectioners' sugar, 2 tablespoons
soft butter, 1 teaspoon grated orange rind, and enough orange juice to thin frosting to spreading consistency. MAKES
36 TO 40.

NOTE: 3/4 cup milk soured with 1 teaspoon vinegar or
lemon juice may be substituted for the sour cream. In
that case, increase butter to 1/2 cup.

NANCY BURR: *"I got this recipe from my friend Dora
Ferguson. She was a caterer in Quincy, Massachusetts,
and I think her company is still in business even though
Dora is deceased."*

PINEAPPLE CHEESECAKE BARS

1/2 cup cold butter
1 1/4 cups flour
1/3 cup sugar
1 tablespoon grated orange
  rind
8 ounces cream cheese,
  softened

1/4 cup sugar
1 egg
1 tablespoon lemon juice
1/2 cup chopped candied
  pineapple

Cut cold butter into chunks and place in mixing bowl. Add flour, 1/3 cup sugar, and grated orange rind. Beat at low speed or by hand until well mixed. Set aside 1/2 cup of the mixture, and press the remainder into an ungreased 8" square pan. Bake at 350°F for 12 to 17 minutes, until edges are lightly browned. Meanwhile, using same bowl, combine cream cheese, 1/4 cup sugar, egg, and lemon juice, and mix until light and fluffy. Stir in candied pineapple. Spread filling over hot crust. Sprinkle with reserved crumb mixture. Return to oven and bake for an additional 15 to 20 minutes. Cool completely, then cut into bars. Store covered in refrigerator. MAKES ABOUT 24.

SUSAN MAHNKE PEERY

PAUL'S PUMPKIN BARS

◆————————————————————◆

4 eggs
1 2/3 cups sugar
1 cup vegetable oil
1 16-ounce can pumpkin
2 cups flour
2 teaspoons baking
  powder
2 teaspoons cinnamon

1 teaspoon salt
1 teaspoon baking soda
1 3-ounce package cream
  cheese, softened
1/2 cup butter, softened
1 teaspoon vanilla
2 cups confectioners'
  sugar

In mixing bowl, beat together eggs, sugar, oil, and pumpkin until light and fluffy. Stir together flour, baking powder, cinnamon, salt, and baking soda, and add to pumpkin mixture. Mix thoroughly. Spread batter in ungreased 15" x 10" x 1" baking pan. Bake at 350°F for 25 to 30 minutes. Cool. Make icing: Combine cream cheese and butter. Add vanilla, and beat in confectioners' sugar until mixture is smooth. Frost cooled bars. MAKES 48.

MARY BEVILACQUA: *"I took a fancy to the name of these bars, because my son's name is Paul. These are as special as he is."*

RHUBARB BARS

1 cup flour
5 tablespoons confection-
ers' sugar
1/2 cup butter
2 eggs
1 1/2 cups sugar

1/4 cup flour
1/4 teaspoon baking pow-
der
1/2 teaspoon salt
2 cups chopped rhubarb

Blend 1 cup flour, confectioners' sugar, and butter. Pat into 9″ x 13″ pan. Bake at 350°F for about 20 minutes. Blend eggs and sugar. Add 1/4 cup flour, baking powder, and salt. Mix well. Fold in the rhubarb. Pour over crust and bake for 35 minutes. Cut into bars when cool. MAKES ABOUT 48.

JEAN DE LONGCHAMP

8. TEA PARTY FANCIES:
The Perfect Cookie to Serve with a Cup of Tea or Coffee

VIENNESE SANDWICH COOKIES

Dough:
1 cup butter
1 cup sugar
1 egg yolk

1 teaspoon vanilla
2 cups flour

Filling:
1/2 cup butter
2 cups confectioners' sugar

2 to 4 tablespoons lemon juice

Dip:
4 ounces semi-sweet chocolate

2 tablespoons butter
Colored nonpareils

Cream butter well and gradually add sugar. Add egg yolk and vanilla. Blend in flour. Chill dough for at least 1 hour. After dough has chilled, roll it into 72 walnut-size balls. Place on greased cookie sheets and flatten with the bottom of a glass dipped in sugar. (Or roll chilled dough out onto greased cookie sheets and cut into circles using 1 1/2" cookie cutter.) Press to about 1/8" thickness. Bake at 325°F for 8 to 10 minutes. Remove from sheets and allow to cool on rack.

To prepare filling: Cream butter and confectioners' sugar. Mix in lemon juice. Beat to spreading consistency.

Frost the underside of half of the cookies with lemon filling. Press another cookie on top to form a sandwich. Prepare chocolate dip by melting chocolate with butter. Stir well. Holding each cookie sandwich firmly, dip one half into the chocolate and then into the nonpareils. Place on racks to let chocolate harden. MAKES 36 SANDWICHES.

MAUREEN ROBINSON

MOCHA NUT BUTTER COOKIES

1 cup butter, softened
1/2 cup sugar
2 teaspoons instant coffee
1 tablespoon water
2 teaspoons vanilla
1 3/4 cups flour
1/4 cup unsweetened
cocoa powder
1/2 teaspoon salt
2 cups finely chopped
pecans or walnuts
Confectioners' sugar

Cream butter and sugar in a large bowl. Dissolve instant coffee in water and stir into butter mixture. Add vanilla. Sift flour, cocoa, and salt into butter mixture. Beat until smooth. Blend in nuts. Shape dough into 1″ balls and place on greased cookie sheets about 1″ apart. Bake at 325°F for 15 minutes. Cool on wire racks. Roll in confectioners' sugar and store in an airtight container. MAKES 3 DOZEN.

MAUREEN ROBINSON: *"The flavor of these cookies is unusual and they melt in your mouth. The recipe comes from my mother."*

MOCHA NUT MERINGUE DROPS

3 large egg whites
1/4 teaspoon cream of tartar
Pinch of salt
3/4 cup sugar
1/2 cup cocoa

2 teaspoons very strong coffee (either make brewed coffee, or mix 1/2 teaspoon instant coffee with 2 teaspoons boiling water)
1 cup chopped walnuts

In large bowl, combine egg whites, cream of tartar, and salt, and beat until soft peaks form. Gradually add sugar, about 2 tablespoons at a time, and beat until peaks are firm. Fold in cocoa and coffee, then fold in nuts. Drop by rounded teaspoonfuls onto ungreased cookie sheet lined with brown paper, or put batter into a pastry bag and pipe through a wide tube into decorative shapes. Bake at 275°F until set and dry, about 45 minutes. Store in an airtight container. MAKES ABOUT 6 DOZEN.

NANCY PLATTS: *"Do not attempt to make these in humid weather. Do not use a plastic bowl to beat the egg whites, and be sure all utensils are completely free of any grease or oil, as these will seriously affect the volume of the egg whites. To vary this recipe and make chocolate nut meringue drops, use 2 teaspoons vanilla in place of coffee."*

CHOCOLATE BUTTER SWEETS

◆━━━━━━━━━━━━━━━━━━━━━━━━━━━━━━━━━━━◆

Dough:
1/2 cup butter
1/2 cup confectioners'
  sugar
1/4 teaspoon salt

1 teaspoon vanilla
1 1/4 cups sifted flour
1/4 teaspoon baking
  powder

Filling:
3 ounces cream cheese,
  softened
1 cup confectioners' sugar
2 tablespoons flour

1 teaspoon vanilla
1/2 cup coconut
1/2 cup chopped pecans

Frosting:
1/2 cup chocolate chips
2 tablespoons butter
2 tablespoons water

3/4 cup confectioners'
  sugar

Cream butter and sugar. Add salt and vanilla. Mix well. Add flour and baking powder gradually. Roll into 3/4" balls. Place on lightly greased cookie sheets and flatten with the bottom of a glass dipped in sugar. Bake at 350°F for 10 to 12 minutes.

While cookies are baking, prepare filling by combining cream cheese, sugar, flour, and vanilla. Mix well. Stir in coconut and pecans. Place 1 teaspoonful on top of each warm cookie.

To prepare frosting: Heat chocolate, butter, and water over low heat until chocolate melts. Add sugar and beat until smooth. Cool slightly. Drizzle small amount of frosting over each cookie. MAKES ABOUT 30.

MAUREEN ROBINSON: *"This recipe came from Pat Pepper, who taught a delightful Holiday Gift-Giving class in Dover for several years before she moved to California. It is an old southern recipe that she has been making for years, and it is delicious!"*

SNOWFLAKE CHEESE TARTS

Dough:

2 cups flour
1/4 teaspoon salt
1 teaspoon sugar
1 cup butter

1/2 cup sour cream
1 egg yolk
Confectioners' sugar

Cheese filling:

8 ounces cream cheese
1 egg
1/2 cup sugar

1 teaspoon vanilla
1 teaspoon finely grated
  lemon rind

For dough, combine flour, salt, and sugar. Cut in butter until uniform pea-sized lumps form. Combine egg yolk and sour cream and incorporate into flour-butter mixture until a cohesive dough forms. Knead lightly for a minute or two, then divide into 3 parts. Wrap each separately and chill. Roll out on floured pastry cloth to approximately 9" × 12" rectangle. Cut into 3" squares. For cheese filling, combine all ingredients and beat until smooth. Place 1 teaspoon filling in center of each square just before fitting pastry into small ungreased tartlet pans (3/4" deep x 1 1/2" wide). Bake at 375°F for 25 to 30 minutes. Cool on wire rack before dusting lightly with confectioners' sugar. MAKES 2 1/2 TO 3 DOZEN.

LAUREL GABEL

VANILLA CRESCENTS

1 cup sweet butter
1/3 cup sugar
1 teaspoon vanilla
1/2 teaspoon almond
 extract
1 3/4 cups flour

Pinch of salt
1/2 cup blanched, ground
 almonds
Confectioners' sugar for
 dusting

Cream butter and sugar. Add vanilla and almond extract and beat well. Stir in flour, salt, and ground almonds. Mix well and form a firm ball. Chill for 1/2 hour. Shape into thin cylinders. Cut off 1" lengths and form into crescents. Bake on ungreased cookie sheets at 325°F for about 7 to 10 minutes. Cookies should remain light in color. Dust with confectioners' sugar while warm and remove gently from cookie sheets. These cookies keep well. MAKES ABOUT 48.

MONICA FORMAN

RICH BUTTER WAFERS

1 cup butter
1 cup sugar
1 egg

1 teaspoon vanilla
2 cups sifted flour

Cream butter until very soft. Add sugar gradually, beating until light and fluffy. Beat in egg, then add vanilla. Add flour and mix well. Roll dough into 3/4" balls. Place on greased cookie sheets. Press each ball with a flat-bottomed glass dipped in granulated sugar. Bake at 375°F until edges are light brown, about 8 to 10 minutes. MAKES 3 DOZEN.

WINNIE ODELL

ALMOND NUT COOKIES

1/2 cup sweet butter
1/2 cup sugar
1 egg yolk
1 teaspoon vanilla

1 cup sifted flour
3/4 cup toasted, chopped
    almonds
1 tablespoon cognac

Cream butter and sugar. Beat in egg yolk, vanilla, and flour. Mix in nuts and cognac. Drop teaspoonfuls of batter onto greased and floured cookie sheets. Bake at 300°F for 20 to 25 minutes, until light golden. Remove to wire racks to cool. MAKES ABOUT 30.

SUSAN MAHNKE PEERY: *"These cookies are delicate and fragrant."*

APRICOT WALNUT CRESCENTS

2 cups flour
Dash of salt
1 teaspoon sugar
1 cup butter
1 cup sour cream
1 egg, lightly beaten

6 tablespoons apricot
  preserves
6 tablespoons ground
  walnuts
Confectioners' sugar

Mix flour, salt, and sugar. With a pastry blender, cut butter into flour until mixture resembles coarse crumbs. Stir in sour cream and egg. Knead lightly until mixture holds together. Wrap well in plastic wrap and refrigerate for 4 hours or overnight. Divide dough into thirds. On a lightly floured pastry cloth, roll each third into a circle 11" in diameter. Spread each circle evenly with 2 tablespoons of apricot preserves and 2 tablespoons grou.d walnuts. Cut each circle into 12 pie-shaped wedges. Roll up each wedge, starting at the wide end. Place seam-side down about 2" apart on greased cookie sheets. Bake at 375°F for 20 minutes, until golden brown. Place on wire rack. Dust with confectioners' sugar when completely cool. MAKES 3 DOZEN.

LAUREL GABEL

CARDAMOM COOKIES

1 cup butter
2 teaspoons baking soda
1 teaspoon ground carda-
  mom
1/2 teaspoon salt
1/2 cup light brown sugar,
  firmly packed

2 eggs
4 1/2 cups flour
2 teaspoons cream of
  tartar

Cream butter and add baking soda, cardamom, and salt. Mix well. Blend in sugar. Beat in eggs. Sift together flour and cream of tartar and stir into butter mixture, blending well. Chill for 3 or 4 hours, or overnight. Shape dough into 1/2″ balls. Place on ungreased cookie sheets. Dip a fork into flour and press each cookie crisscross style. Bake at 350°F for about 10 minutes. MAKES ABOUT 48.

WINNIE ODELL

BUTTER HORNS

1 pint sour cream
2 eggs, separated

1 pound butter, melted
4 cups flour

Filling:

2 cups sugar (or to taste)
2 cups chopped walnuts

1 tablespoon cinnamon

Mix sour cream and egg yolks. Add melted butter and stir until blended. Add flour and mix well. Dough will be soft—somewhere between a batter and a dough. Chill, covered, overnight, until the consistency of soft fudge.

Combine all filling ingredients. Divide chilled dough into 8 parts, and keep refrigerated while working with one part at a time. Roll each part into a circle, about 12" in diameter. Sprinkle with 1/8 of the filling. Cut into 12 or 16 wedges. Use a pastry wheel to crimp the edges. Roll up each wedge, starting at the wide end. Place on ungreased cookie sheets. Brush tops with lightly beaten egg whites. Bake at 350°F for 10 to 15 minutes. MAKES ABOUT 72.

MICHELINA PRENCIPE: *"These high-caloried and delicious cookies were introduced to me by my dear Aunt Helen."*

BANBURY TARTS

Pastry for a double pie
 crust
One 28-ounce jar mince-
 meat
1 large apple, peeled,
 cored, and thinly sliced

4 ounces sharp cheddar
 cheese, grated
1 egg yolk
1 tablespoon water

Roll out pieces of pie crust. Cut into 4" squares. Place equal amounts of mincemeat and sliced apples in the center of each square. Top with about 1 tablespoon of grated cheese. Fold each square on the diagonal to make a triangle. Press edges together with floured fork tines. Cut small slits in top of each crust. Beat egg yolk and water and brush over tarts. Place on cookie sheets. Bake at 425°F for 10 to 12 minutes, until golden brown. Can be served warm or cold. MAKES ABOUT 25.

> JACKIE FITZPATRICK: *"You can make smaller tarts, about 3" square. To do this, you may have to make extra pie crust dough."*

CRÈME DE MENTHE BARS

Dough:

4 ounces unsweetened
   chocolate
2/3 cup oil
2 cups brown sugar,
   firmly packed

3 eggs
1 1/4 cups flour
1/2 teaspoon baking soda
1/4 teaspoon salt
1 teaspoon vanilla

Filling:

4 cups confectioners'
   sugar
3/4 cup butter
3 tablespoons crème de
   menthe, or 2 teaspoons
   peppermint extract

3 tablespoons milk or
   cream
Green food coloring

Topping:

6 ounces (1 cup) semi-
   sweet chocolate bits

3 tablespoons oil

To make dough: Melt chocolate with oil in top of large double boiler, or over low heat in a heavy saucepan. Add brown sugar and eggs and mix well. Stir in flour, baking soda, salt, and vanilla, and mix well. Spread in greased 15" x 10" x 1" jelly-roll pan. Bake at 350°F for 15 to 20 minutes. Cool completely.

To make filling: Blend confectioners' sugar and butter until creamy. Add crème de menthe or peppermint, milk, and a few drops of green food coloring. Mix well. Spread evenly over cooled chocolate base. Refrigerate.

To make topping: Combine chocolate bits and oil in top of double boiler until completely melted. Spread carefully over green filling. It will take an hour or more for the topping to become firm. Refrigerate if weather is warm. Cut into small squares. Each square may be served in a small cupcake paper. MAKES ABOUT 100 1" X 1 1/2" SQUARES.

NANCY PLATTS

PECAN TARTLETS

Pastry Shells:
1/2 cup butter
3 ounces cream cheese

1 cup flour

Filling:
2 tablespoons butter
1/4 cup dark brown sugar,
  firmly packed
1/2 teaspoon vanilla

1 egg
1/3 cup dark corn syrup or
  maple syrup
1 cup pecan halves

Cream butter and cream cheese. Work in flour. Wrap dough and chill for several hours. Roll into 24 balls (about the size of ripe olives) and press each ball into and up the sides of ungreased small muffin tins (about 1 3/4" across the top). If kitchen is warm, refrigerate shells until filling is ready.

To prepare filling: Cream butter, sugar, and vanilla. Beat in egg, then add syrup, blending well. Stir in pecans.

Fill unbaked pastry shells about 3/4 full with mixture. Bake at 375°F for 20 minutes. Cool briefly in pan on wire rack, then remove tartlets from pan and cool completely. MAKES 24.

NANCY PLATTS

RICE JAM CAKES

1/2 cup butter
1 cup sugar
2 eggs
1 tablespoon milk
1 teaspoon almond extract
1 teaspoon baking powder
1 cup rice flour

Enough pie pastry to
make 2 double-crust
pies (or 2 boxes of pie-
crust mix, prepared)
1 13-ounce jar raspberry
jam

Cream butter, sugar, and eggs. Beat well. Add milk and almond extract. Add baking powder and rice flour and mix until well blended. Roll out pie crust dough and cut out 60 circles to fit 2" tartlet pans, greased. Add 1 level teaspoon of jam to each tart and top with 1 teaspoon of rice flour batter. Make sure jam is completely covered. Bake at 450°F for 8 to 10 minutes. Cool and remove cakes from pans. MAKES 60.

MARY BEVILACQUA: *"This is an old English recipe, a favorite at teatime. It was given to me by one of my nursing students whose grandmother came from England. The rice flour adds an unusual crunch to these little cakes."*

WINE BISCUITS

4 cups flour
5 teaspoons baking
  powder
1/2 teaspoon salt
3/4 cup sugar

1 teaspoon aniseed
3/4 cup oil
1 cup sherry or muscatel
  wine

Sift together dry ingredients. Add aniseed, oil, and wine, and mix well. Roll into thin ropes about 4″ long and shape or twist as desired. Place on ungreased cookie sheets. Bake at 350°F for 20 minutes, until brown. MAKES ABOUT 55 BISCUITS.

CHRIS COPPOLINO

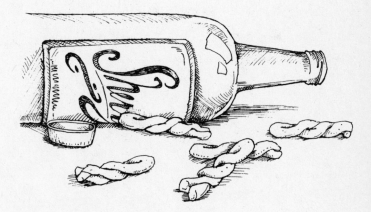

OATIES

1 cup flour
2 teaspoons baking
  powder
1/2 teaspoon salt
1 cup rolled oats

1/4 cup molasses
1/2 cup butter
1/4 cup sugar
1 tablespoon rolled oats
  for topping

In a bowl, combine flour, baking powder, and salt. Stir in rolled oats. Place molasses, butter, and sugar in a small saucepan over very low heat, and stir until butter is melted and mixture is smooth. Add butter mixture to dry mixture. Pat dough into a buttered 8" pie pan. Score dough into 8 wedges and sprinkle with remaining tablespoon of rolled oats. Bake at 350°F for 20 to 25 minutes, until firm. Serve warm with marmalade and a proper cup of tea. SERVES 8.

SUSAN MAHNKE PEERY

9. CHRISTMAS COOKIES:
Traditional Favorites for
the Holidays

MELTING MOMENTS

1 cup flour
1/2 cup confectioners'
  sugar

2 tablespoons cornstarch
1 cup butter, softened
1 1/3 cups shredded coco-
  nut

Mix flour, sugar, and cornstarch. Blend in butter to make a soft dough. Chill for at least 1/2 hour. Shape into small balls and roll in coconut to cover. Place 2″ apart on ungreased cookie sheets and bake at 300°F for 20 to 25 minutes, until coconut is golden. MAKES ABOUT 3 DOZEN.

MARY BEVILACQUA

ALMOND CRESCENT COOKIES

1/2 cup butter
1/3 cup confectioners'
  sugar
1/2 teaspoon vanilla
1/4 teaspoon almond
  extract

3/4 cup plus 2 tablespoons
  flour
1/8 teaspoon salt
1/2 cup chopped, blanched
  almonds

Cream butter and sugar. Stir in flavorings, flour, and salt. Add almonds. Roll teaspoonfuls of dough into 2″ ropes and lay them on lightly greased cookie sheets. Shape each rope into a crescent. Bake for 15 minutes at 325°F. MAKES 30 TO 36.

MARY BEVILACQUA

NUTMEG NOELS

2 tablespoons red or green
  colored sugar
3/4 teaspoon nutmeg
1 1/2 cups flour
3/4 cup sugar
1 teaspoon cream of tartar

1/2 teaspoon baking soda
1/8 teaspoon salt
1/2 cup butter, softened
1 egg
1 teaspoon vanilla

Combine colored sugar and 1/4 teaspoon of the nutmeg in a small bowl and set aside. Place flour, sugar, cream of tartar, baking soda, and salt in a mixing bowl. Add remaining 1/4 teaspoon nutmeg. Stir together. Add butter, egg, and vanilla and mix well, beating with an electric mixer on low speed if desired. Form dough into 1" balls and roll in sugar-nutmeg mixture. Place about 2" apart on ungreased cookie sheets and bake at 400°F for 10 to 12 minutes, until firm. Cool on wire racks. MAKES ABOUT 40.

MARY BEVILACQUA

LEMON SNOWBALLS

1 cup sweet butter
1/2 cup confectioners'
  sugar
1 1/2 cups flour
3/4 cup cornstarch
1/4 teaspoon salt

2 teaspoons grated lemon
  rind
1 cup finely chopped
  toasted blanched
  almonds

Frosting:
1 cup confectioners' sugar
2 tablespoons melted
  sweet butter

1 tablespoon lemon juice

Cream butter and sugar. Add flour sifted with cornstarch and salt. Mix in the lemon rind. Shape into 1" balls and roll in chopped nuts, pressing the nuts into the dough. Bake for about 15 minutes at 350°F on greased cookie sheets. Cool on wire rack.

In a small bowl, combine frosting ingredients. Beat until smooth and drizzle over cookies. MAKES ABOUT 2 DOZEN.

LAUREL GABEL

HIDDEN KISSES

1 cup butter
1/2 cup confectioners'
  sugar
1 teaspoon vanilla
2 cups flour
1 cup finely chopped nuts

One 5 3/4-ounce package
  (approx. 40) chocolate
  kisses, with foil re-
  moved
Confectioners' sugar for
  rolling

With a mixer at medium speed, blend butter, sugar, and vanilla until light and fluffy. At low speed, beat in flour and nuts until well blended. Divide dough into 40 parts. Shape each part around a chocolate kiss, covering it completely. Bake on an ungreased cookie sheet for 12 minutes at 375°F. The cookies do not brown. Let stand for one minute. Remove to rack, cool slightly, and roll in confectioners' sugar. When completely cool, roll in confectioners' sugar again. MAKES 40.

LAUREL GABEL

MELTAWAYS

1 cup butter
1/2 cup sugar
1/2 cup brown sugar,
  firmly packed
1 egg
2 1/4 cups flour

1 teaspoon cream of tartar
2 teaspoons baking soda
1/2 teaspoon salt
Sugar for rolling

Cream butter and sugars. Add egg and mix well. Sift together flour, cream of tartar, baking soda, and salt, and add to butter mixture. Chill dough if necessary for handling. Shape into small balls and roll in sugar, then place on ungreased cookie sheets and bake at 350°F for 10 to 12 minutes. MAKES 4 DOZEN.

SUSAN MAHNKE PEERY: *"I got this recipe during college days in Wisconsin from my friend Linda Dirkse, who now lives in Bakersfield, California."*

SACHER TORTE COOKIES

1 cup butter, softened
1 package (4 1/2-ounce
  size) instant chocolate
  pudding mix
1 egg
1 teaspoon almond extract
2 cups flour

3 tablespoons sugar
1/2 cup apricot preserves
1/2 cup semi-sweet choco-
  late chips
3 tablespoons butter,
  melted

Preheat oven to 325°F. In a large mixing bowl combine butter and pudding mix; cream together until fluffy. Beat in egg and almond extract. Gradually add flour, beating at low speed with mixer until dough forms. Shape into 1" balls. Roll balls in sugar. Place 2" apart on ungreased cookie sheets. With your thumb, make an imprint in the center of each cookie. Bake for 15 to 18 minutes or until cookies are firm: remove from cookie sheets immediately. Cool. Fill each indentation with 1/2 teaspoon of preserves. In a small saucepan blend chips and butter over low heat until chocolate melts, stirring constantly. Drizzle 1/2 teaspoon chocolate over each cookie. MAKES ABOUT 36.

MAUREEN ROBINSON

ITALIAN HOLIDAY COOKIES

1 cup sweet butter
1/3 cup sugar
1 egg yolk
1/4 teaspoon vanilla
1 1/2 cups flour

1 egg white, slightly
 beaten
1 cup shredded coconut
Fruit preserves

Cream together butter and sugar until light and fluffy. Stir in egg yolk and vanilla. Add flour to creamed mixture and blend thoroughly. Chill dough for at least 1 hour. Shape dough into 3/4" balls, dip balls in egg white, and then roll balls lightly in coconut. Place on an ungreased cookie sheet. Press gently on top of each ball with your thumb to form an indentation. Bake in a 325°F oven for 20 to 25 minutes. Cool. Fill centers with preserves. MAKES ABOUT 30.

MARY ANN GROME

LEMON NUTMEG MELTAWAYS

1 cup sifted cake flour
1/2 cup cornstarch
1/4 teaspoon salt
1/2 teaspoon nutmeg
10 tablespoons unsalted
  butter, softened

1/2 cup confectioners'
  sugar
2 teaspoons grated lemon
  rind

Sift dry ingredients onto waxed paper. Beat butter, sugar, and lemon rind in mixer until light and fluffy. Add dry ingredients. Beat on low speed until mixture is smooth. Shape teaspoonfuls of dough into balls and place on an ungreased baking sheet. Flatten slightly to 1 1/4" circles with the bottom of a glass dipped in confectioners' sugar. Bake at 325°F for 15 minutes or until golden brown around the edges. Cool for 2 minutes on cookie sheet and then transfer to a wire rack to finish cooling. MAKES 36.

MARY BEVILACQUA

BUTTER PECAN BALLS

1 cup butter
2 tablespoons sugar
1/4 cup light molasses
  (not blackstrap)
2 cups flour

1/2 teaspoon salt
2 cups finely chopped
  pecans
Confectioners' sugar for
  rolling

In a large mixing bowl, cream butter and sugar. Add molasses and blend well. Gradually add flour and salt and mix well. Stir in nuts. Shape into 1" balls and place on lightly greased cookie sheets. Bake at 350°F for 20 to 25 minutes. Roll in confectioners' sugar while still warm. MAKES 4 DOZEN.

MARY BEVILACQUA: *"I like the hint of molasses in these cookies. They seem to melt away!"*

PINK LEMONADE SQUARES

One 7-ounce package va-
  nilla wafers
1/2 cup butter, melted
One 6-ounce can frozen
  pink lemonade concen-
  trate

3/4 cup water
48 large marshmallows
1 cup heavy cream

Crush vanilla wafers into crumbs and mix with melted butter. Reserve 1/2 cup of the crumb mixture and press the remainder onto the bottom and sides of an 8" x 8" pan. Bake at 325°F for 15 minutes. Cool on rack. Combine lemonade concentrate and water. In a saucepan, heat slowly until mixture is hot. Add marshmallows and continue stirring until marshmallows melt and mixture is smooth. Chill for 1 hour, until thickened. Beat cream until stiff and fold into marshmallow mixture. Spoon onto cooled crust and sprinkle with 1/2 cup reserved crumbs. Freeze until firm. MAKES 16 TO 20.

MARY BEVILACQUA: *"I heard this recipe on Gus Saunder's 'Yankee Kitchen,' a Boston radio show. It is more a light dessert than a packageable cookie. You can decorate the squares with green candied cherries for a more festive look."*

SUGAR PLUMS

3/4 cup butter
1/2 cup confectioners'
  sugar
1/4 teaspoon salt
1 3/4 cups flour
1 6-ounce package
  butterscotch chips

1 cup finely chopped
  pecans
Rum glaze (see below)
Green and red candied
  cherries
Pecan halves

Rum glaze:
2 cups sifted confectioners'
  sugar

1/4 cup light rum

Cream butter until smooth; add sugar and salt and mix together well. Stir in flour and blend well. Add chips and nuts. Shape into balls about the size of a small walnut. Place 1″ apart on cookie sheets. Bake at 325°F for 15 to 20 minutes until firm but not brown. Cool completely on racks.

Combine sugar and rum and stir until smooth. Spoon glaze over cool cookies. Decorate with cherry halves and pecan halves. Use small "leaves" of green cherries around a red half cherry. MAKES 4 TO 5 DOZEN.

JACKIE ROGERS: *"This is my annual cookie for the Cookie Exchange—a tradition."*

TOASTED ALMOND FINGERS

1 cup butter
1/2 cup confectioners'
  sugar
1 tablespoon milk
1 teaspoon vanilla
1/4 teaspoon salt
2 cups sifted flour

2 cups finely chopped,
  toasted slivered
  almonds
6 ounces (1 cup) chocolate
  chips
2 tablespoons vegetable
  shortening

Beat butter and sugar until light. Beat in milk, vanilla, and salt. At low speed, beat in flour. Stir in chopped almonds. Wrap dough in waxed paper and refrigerate until firm. Shape small pieces of dough into 2″ fingers. Bake at 350°F on ungreased cookie sheets for 15 minutes. Cool on wire rack. In double boiler, melt chocolate chips and shortening over hot water. Carefully dip one end of each cookie into frosting, and let harden on rack or waxed paper. These cookies freeze well. MAKES ABOUT 40.

LAUREL GABEL

NUTMEG LOGS

1 cup butter, softened
3/4 cup sugar
1 egg
2 teaspoons vanilla

2 2/3 cups flour
1 teaspoon freshly grated
   nutmeg (more to taste)
1/4 teaspoon salt

Frosting:
2 tablespoons butter,
   softened
1 1/4 cups confectioners'
   sugar

2 to 3 tablespoons light
   rum or 1 teaspoon rum
   flavoring plus 2 tablespoons milk

Cream butter and gradually add sugar, creaming until light and fluffy. Beat in egg and vanilla. Mix together flour, nutmeg, and salt and add to butter mixture. Mix well. On a lightly floured surface, roll pieces of dough by hand into long ropes 1/2" in diameter. Cut ropes into 3" pieces and place the segments 1" apart on ungreased cookie sheets. Bake at 350°F for 12 to 15 minutes, until firm but not browned. Cool on racks. Prepare frosting by creaming the butter, sugar, and rum. Add more rum if necessary to reach a creamy consistency. Spread cookies with frosting and mark with tines of fork to resemble bark. MAKES ABOUT 66.

MARY BEVILACQUA

LEMON CRESCENTS

1 cup flour
1/2 cup finely chopped
   walnuts
1/2 cup butter, softened
1/3 cup light brown sugar,
   firmly packed

1 egg yolk
1 1/2 teaspoons grated
   lemon rind
Sugar for rolling

Mix flour and walnuts and set aside. Beat butter and brown sugar with electric mixer until pale and fluffy. Beat in egg yolk and lemon rind, and add flour. Chill dough for several hours or overnight. Cut dough into 24 pieces and roll each piece into a 3″ rope. Roll each piece in sugar and place on an ungreased cookie sheet. Bend into crescent shapes. Bake at 325°F for 10 minutes, until firm and lightly browned. Cool on rack. MAKES 24.

SUSAN MAHNKE PEERY

PECAN BUTTERBALLS

1 cup butter
1/2 cup confectioners'
sugar
2 teaspoons vanilla
2 cups sifted flour

1/2 teaspoon salt
1 cup finely chopped pecans
Confectioners' sugar for rolling

Cream butter and 1/2 cup confectioners' sugar. Add vanilla and beat well. Stir in flour, salt, and chopped pecans. Mix well, and chill dough if necessary. Shape in small balls and bake on ungreased cookie sheets for about 15 minutes at 350°F. Remove from pan, cool for a few minutes, and roll carefully in confectioners' sugar. Let cool completely. Dust with additional confectioners' sugar just before serving. MAKES 3 TO 4 DOZEN, DEPENDING ON SIZE.

SUSAN MAHNKE PEERY: *"My mother, Margaret Mahnke, makes these every Christmas, along with many other kinds of cookies."*

GINGERBREAD BOYS

1/2 cup butter
1/2 cup sugar
1/2 cup molasses
1 egg
1 teaspoon baking soda
1 tablespoon milk

1 teaspoon ground ginger
1 teaspoon cinnamon
1/4 teaspoon salt
2 3/4 to 3 cups flour
1 egg white

Butter Frosting:

1/3 cup butter, softened
1 egg yolk
1 cup confectioners' sugar

Vanilla or other flavoring
as desired

Cream butter and sugar. Add molasses and egg and beat well. Dissolve soda in milk and add to batter. Sift together ginger, cinnamon, salt, and flour, and add to batter, mixing thoroughly. Chill dough for at least 24 hours. Roll out fairly thin and cut into gingerbread-boy shapes. Whip egg white with a tablespoon of cold water and glaze cutouts, using a soft-bristled pastry brush. (This gives the boys a shiny surface and covers any imperfections.) Press on candied fruit or nuts for features, if desired. Bake at 350°F for 6 to 8 minutes or longer, until firm but not too brown.

To make frosting: Blend butter and egg yolk until smooth; stir in confectioners' sugar and flavoring. Tint frosting if desired.

Frost and decorate as desired, preferably enlisting the assistance of a small child or two. MAKES AT LEAST 4 DOZEN, DEPENDING ON SIZE OF COOKIE CUTTER.

ELEANOR HOMEYER

GRANDMA'S HOLIDAY
COOKIE CUTOUTS

1 cup butter
2 cups light brown sugar,
  firmly packed
2 eggs, well beaten
1 teaspoon vanilla

4 cups flour
1 teaspoon cream of tartar
1 teaspoon baking soda
Dash of salt

Cream butter and sugar. Add eggs, vanilla, and sifted dry ingredients, mixing well. Chill dough. Roll out on floured pastry cloth to desired thickness—about 1/8" is best. Cut with floured cookie cutters and transfer to lightly greased cookie sheets. Bake at 375°F for 7 or 8 minutes, until lightly browned. Decorate as desired. MAKES 4 TO 6 DOZEN, DEPENDING ON SIZE.

LAUREL GABEL

SUGAR COOKIES

1 cup butter or margarine
1 cup sugar
1 cup confectioners' sugar
2 eggs
1 cup oil
2 teaspoons vanilla

4 1/4 cups unsifted
  flour
1 teaspoon baking soda
1 teaspoon cream of tartar
1/2 teaspoon salt
Colored sugar

In a large bowl with electric mixer at medium speed, cream butter and sugars. Beat in eggs one at a time until mixture is light. Add oil and vanilla. Beat until well blended. In a large bowl, combine flour, baking soda, cream of tartar, and salt. Gradually add dry ingredients to the creamed mixture, and beat until blended. Wrap dough and chill for several hours. Roll teaspoonfuls of dough into balls and place on a greased cookie sheet. Flatten dough to 2" circles with the bottom of a glass dipped in granulated sugar. Sprinkle with colored sugar. Bake at 325°F for 8 to 10 minutes, just until set. Let stand on the cookie sheet for 2 to 3 minutes before removing. MAKES ABOUT 7 DOZEN.

NANCY PLATTS: *"This is my most popular recipe, the one everyone asks for. I use colored sugars at Christmas time, but chocolate sprinkles or cinnamon and sugar may be used during other seasons."*

YUL LOCKA

1/2 cup butter
1 3/4 cups confectioners'
sugar
2 eggs
2 cups Wondra flour

1/4 teaspoon cinnamon
1/2 teaspoon baking
powder
1 1/2 teaspoons grated
lemon rind

Cream butter and sugar thoroughly. Add eggs one at a time, beating well. Stir dry ingredients together and add to butter mixture. Stir in lemon rind, and mix well. Refrigerate overnight. Roll out thin on a lightly floured surface and cut with cookie cutters. Bake at 350°F on lightly greased cookie sheets for 7 to 9 minutes. MAKES ABOUT 4 DOZEN.

JACKIE ROGERS: *"We traditionally use a bell cookie cutter for this thin, crisp Christmas cookie."*

TERESA'S CHRISTMAS COOKIES

2/3 cup butter
1 1/4 cups sugar
2 eggs
3 cups flour
1/2 teaspoon salt

2 teaspoons baking
 powder
1 teaspoon vanilla
1 teaspoon lemon extract
2 tablespoons milk

Cream butter and sugar. Add eggs and beat well. Mix flour, salt, and baking powder together and add, stirring well. Add extracts and milk and mix to a smooth dough. Chill for several hours or overnight. Roll out thin on a lightly floured board and cut with cookie cutters. Bake on un-greased cookie sheets at 350°F for about 10 minutes. MAKES 4 TO 5 DOZEN.

NANCY COPPOLINO: *"This recipe, from my mother, Terry Ouellette, is a tradition in my family. Every year about 2 weeks before Christmas we would help Mom (or Grandma) decorate these lemon shortbreads."*

RICH ROLLED COOKIES

1 cup butter
2/3 cup sugar
1 egg

1 teaspoon vanilla
2 1/2 cups flour
1/2 teaspoon salt

Cream butter and sugar. Beat in egg and vanilla. Add flour and salt. Mix well. Chill dough, covered, for 3 or 4 hours. Preheat oven to 350°F. Roll out dough 1/4″ thick and cut with cookie cutters. Bake for 8 to 10 minutes, or until slightly browned. MAKES 40 TO 50.

JANET MEANY

BEST BUTTER COOKIES

1 cup butter, softened
1 cup sugar
1 egg
2 tablespoons orange juice

1 tablespoon vanilla
2 1/2 cups flour
1 teaspoon baking powder

Cream butter and sugar. Add egg, orange juice, and vanilla, and mix well. Add flour and baking powder. Cover dough and chill for 2 to 3 hours, until firm. Roll out portions of the dough to 1/4″ thick, keeping the rest chilled. Cut as desired with cookie cutters. Sprinkle some of the cookies with colored sugar before baking, if desired. Place on ungreased cookie sheets and bake at 375°F for about 8 minutes, until lightly browned. Cool completely before frosting. MAKES ABOUT 4 DOZEN.

SUSAN MAHNKE PEERY: *"These cookies are crisp and buttery, and they keep well, if you can keep them hidden!"*

CHRISTMAS TEA COOKIES

1/2 cup butter
1/2 cup margarine
2 cups sugar
2 eggs, beaten
1/2 teaspoon baking soda

2 teaspoons baking
  powder
6 cups flour
1/2 cup buttermilk
1 teaspoon vanilla

Cream butter, margarine, and sugar. Add the beaten eggs. Combine baking soda, baking powder, and 1 cup of the flour. Add dry mixture alternately with buttermilk and vanilla to the butter mixture. Add enough of the remaining flour to make a soft dough. Turn out onto a floured board and knead until smooth. Chill dough if it seems sticky. Roll out dough to 1/4" thick and cut into shapes with a sharp knife (to make your own designs) or cookie cutters. Decorate *before* baking with egg yolk paint (recipe below), or as desired. Bake at 350°F until golden brown, about 10 minutes. MAKES 80 TO 100, DEPENDING ON SIZE.

To make Egg Yolk Paint: Mix 1 egg yolk with 1/2 teaspoon water and blend well. Divide liquid among teacups or custard cups and tint with food coloring. Use small paintbrushes to paint designs on cookies before baking. Thin paint if necessary with a few drops of water.

VAL AND ELIZABETH CARROLL *brought these cookies to the 1982 Cookie Exchange. Each cookie was hand painted.*

MARZIPAN COOKIES

1/2 cup butter
1/3 cup sugar

2 egg yolks
1 1/2 cups flour

Topping:

2 egg whites
7 ounces almond paste
1/2 teaspoon rum flavor-
ing

1 tablespoon grenadine
syrup
1 to 2 cups confectioners'
sugar

Cream butter and sugar. Add egg yolks and stir in flour to make a soft dough. Chill for about an hour.

Meanwhile, make topping. Beat egg whites until stiff but not dry. Set aside. With same beater blend almond paste with rum flavoring and grenadine. Add 1 cup powdered sugar. Fold in egg whites. Add additional sugar to make a mixture that will mound.

Roll out dough 1/4" thick and cut into 1 1/2" circles. Place 1/2 teaspoon topping on each round of dough. Bake at 325°F for 10 to 15 minutes. MAKES ABOUT 5 DOZEN.

NOTE: There will be extra topping for another batch later.

GERI KORTEN

SAND TARTS

1 1/4 cups butter
2 cups sugar
2 eggs

4 cups flour
1/2 teaspoon baking soda

Cream butter and sugar until light. Beat in eggs. Sift together flour and soda and add to butter mixture. Chill dough for 2 to 3 hours. Let dough warm slightly at room temperature before using. Roll thin on floured pastry cloth or board. It may be necessary to flour the rolling pin frequently. Cut into desired shapes. If desired, brush tops of cookies with egg white and sprinkle with plain or colored sugar before baking. Bake on ungreased cookie sheets at 375°F for about 8 minutes. MAKES ABOUT 8 DOZEN.

JACKIE FITZPATRICK: *"The butter taste is important in these cookies—do not substitute other kinds of shortening."*

MY MOTHER'S
SUGAR COOKIES

1/2 cup butter
1 cup sugar
2 eggs
1 tablespoon light cream
2 1/2 cups flour
2 teaspoons baking
  powder

1/2 teaspoon salt
1/2 teaspoon nutmeg
1 teaspoon lemon juice
1/2 teaspoon vanilla

Cream butter and sugar. Beat in eggs and cream. Add flour sifted with baking powder, salt, and nutmeg. Then add lemon juice and vanilla, and mix well. Chill dough for at least 1 hour. Roll out thin on a floured board and bake at 350°F for about 8 minutes, until golden. Do not let cookies get too brown. Decorate as desired. MAKES 4 TO 5 DOZEN.

ELEANOR HOMEYER: *"These are better than ordinary sugar cookies because of the flavoring. Decorate with colored sugar, raisins, nuts, pieces of candied fruit. It wouldn't feel right to have Christmas come before baking sugar-cookie bells, stars, trees, and animals for the family."*

OATMEAL CUTOUTS

◆━━━━━━━━━━━━━━━━━━━━━━━━━━━━━◆

1 cup butter
2/3 cup sugar
1 egg

1 teaspoon vanilla
2 1/2 cups flour
1 cup rolled oats

Cream butter and sugar. Add egg and vanilla and mix well. Add flour and oats. Blend to form a dough. Chill for at least 1 hour. Roll out thin and cut into desired shapes with cookie cutters. Bake at 350°F for about 8 minutes. Decorate as desired. MAKES 4 DOZEN.

LOUISE BOLLES: *"I've used this recipe for Christmas cutout cookies ever since I found it in* The Boston Globe *years ago."*

CANDY BAR COOKIES

Dough:
3/4 cup butter
3/4 cup sifted confectioners' sugar
1 teaspoon vanilla

2 tablespoons evaporated
  milk
1/4 teaspoon salt
2 cups flour

Filling:
1/2 pound light caramels
1/4 cup evaporated milk
1/4 cup butter

1 cup confectioners' sugar
1 cup chopped pecans

Icing:
1 cup semi-sweet
  chocolate bits
1/4 cup evaporated milk

2 tablespoons butter
1 teaspoon vanilla
1/2 cup confectioners'
  sugar

To make dough: Cream butter, adding confectioners' sugar gradually. Add vanilla, evaporated milk, and salt. Mix well. Blend in flour. Roll out dough in two batches, to 1/8" thickness. Cut into 2" squares. Place on ungreased cookie sheets and bake at 325°F for 12 to 15 minutes, until golden. Cool. Spread filling on each square. Top with icing and decorate with pecan halves. MAKES ABOUT 36.

To make filling: Combine caramels and milk in top of double boiler and heat over simmering water until caramels melt, stirring occasionally. Remove from heat. Add butter and confectioners' sugar and mix well. Stir in pecans. Keep warm over hot water.

To make icing: Melt chocolate pieces with evaporated

milk over very low heat. Remove from heat and stir in butter, vanilla, and confectioners' sugar, mixing until smooth.

MARILYN SICURELLA

SPRITZ

1 cup butter
1/2 cup sugar
2 1/4 cups flour
1/4 teaspoon salt

1 egg
1 teaspoon almond or
   vanilla extract

Cream butter and sugar. Blend in remaining ingredients. Fill cookie press with one-quarter of the dough at a time, keeping remaining dough chilled. Form into desired shapes on an ungreased cookie sheet. Bake at 350°F for 6 to 9 minutes, or until set but not browned. MAKES ABOUT 4 DOZEN.

For Chocolate Spritz, add 2 ounces melted unsweetened chocolate to the creamed butter and sugar, and use vanilla extract. Proceed as above.

JANET MEANY: *"This is a traditional Christmas cookie. I press the dough into wreaths and decorate with pieces of red and green candied fruit."*

SPRITZ II

1 cup butter
1 cup margarine
1 1/2 cups sugar
2 eggs
1 teaspoon almond extract

1 teaspoon lemon extract
1 teaspoon vanilla
5 cups flour
1/4 teaspoon salt

Cream butter and margarine, adding sugar gradually. Add eggs and beat well. Add extracts. Add flour and salt and mix well. Fill cookie press with dough (keeping dough chilled until used) and form cookies onto ungreased cookie sheets. Bake at 350°F for 10 to 12 minutes. MAKES AT LEAST 10 DOZEN.

MARY BEVILACQUA

SPRITZ CHOCOLATE SANDWICHES

1 cup butter
1 1/4 cups confectioners' sugar
1 egg

1 teaspoon vanilla
2 1/2 cups flour
1/2 teaspoon salt

Buttery Chocolate Frosting:
3 tablespoons butter
1 1/2 ounces melted unsweetened chocolate
3/4 teaspoon vanilla
1/8 teaspoon salt

3 1/2 cups confectioners' sugar
6 tablespoons light cream or evaporated milk
Chopped walnuts for dipping

Beat butter until light; gradually cream in sugar. Beat in egg and vanilla and blend well. Add flour and salt gradually, and mix well. Using the "star" plate in a cookie press, pipe one-quarter of the dough into 2 1/2" lengths onto an ungreased cookie sheet. Repeat with remaining dough. Bake at 375°F for 6 to 8 minutes, until light brown. Cool on rack.

To prepare frosting: Beat butter until light; add chocolate, vanilla, salt, and confectioners' sugar. Add cream and mix well to make a smooth frosting.

Spread chocolate frosting on flat sides of half the cookies and put a mate to the cookie on top to make a sandwich. Dip the ends of the sandwich into the frosting and then dip the ends into chopped walnuts. MAKES ABOUT 6 DOZEN.

MAUREEN ZOCK: *"This recipe was given to me by Sarah Tathem of Plymouth, New Hampshire. She makes them each spring for the piano recital given at my home in Ashland, New Hampshire, by Mrs. Edith Pryor. They are the first cookies to disappear from the refreshment table."*

CHOCOLATE-GLAZED
OATMEAL SHORTBREAD

2 cups flour
1 cup rolled oats
1/2 teaspoon salt
1 cup butter, softened
1 cup confectioners' sugar
2 teaspoons vanilla

1 cup (6 ounces) semi-
  sweet chocolate chips
1 teaspoon vegetable
  shortening
1 cup finely chopped nuts

Combine flour, oats, and salt, and set aside. In a large bowl, cream butter with confectioners' sugar. Add vanilla and beat until light. Gradually blend in flour-oat mixture. Shape into 2″ logs, using about 1 teaspoonful of dough for each cookie. Bake on ungreased cookie sheets at 325°F for 20 to 25 minutes. Cool on cookie sheets for 1 minute to firm up, then cool completely on racks. Make a chocolate glaze by melting chocolate chips and vegetable shortening together in double boiler over hot water. Stir until smooth. Dip ends of cookies into glaze and then into the chopped nuts. Place on waxed paper to harden before serving. MAKES ABOUT 50.

SUSAN MAHNKE PEERY

RUBY ALMOND COOKIES

1/2 cup butter
1/2 cup sugar
1 teaspoon vanilla
1 egg, separated

1 1/2 cups flour
2/3 cup finely chopped almonds
Raspberry jam

Cream butter and sugar. Add vanilla and egg yolk and beat until fluffy. Stir in flour. Gather dough into a ball, wrap in plastic, and chill for at least 2 hours. Roll level teaspoonfuls of dough into balls. Dip balls into lightly beaten egg white, then roll balls in almonds. Place on ungreased cookie sheet 1" apart. Make an indentation in each ball with your finger or a thimble, and fill with raspberry jam. Bake at 300°F for 20 minutes or until golden. Cool on wire rack. MAKES ABOUT 2 DOZEN.

SUSAN MAHNKE PEERY

SHORTBREAD

1 cup butter, softened
1/2 cup light brown sugar, firmly packed
1/2 teaspoon vanilla

2 cups flour (cake flour or all-purpose)
Unblanched almonds (approx. 3 dozen) (optional)

In a large bowl cream the butter with brown sugar and vanilla until light. Gradually stir in flour until just blended. Chill dough for 30 minutes or until firm. Divide in half. On an ungreased cookie sheet, pat each half into an even circle about 7" in diameter. Prick dough with a fork at 1/2" intervals in a decorative pattern, and use fork tines dipped in flour to make a decorative border around the edges. If desired, press almonds into the dough 1/2" from the edge, about 1" apart. Cover dough with waxed paper and chill for several hours or overnight. Bake at 325°F for 25 to 30 minutes, until firm. Dough should still be pale. Cool on cookie sheets on a rack. Carefully remove to cardboard circles cut to fit. To serve, cut each shortbread into 8 wedges. MAKES 16 WEDGES.

SUSAN MAHNKE PEERY

HOLIDAY MERINGUE COOKIES

2 egg whites
1/8 teaspoon salt
1/8 teaspoon cream of
  tartar
3/4 cup sugar
1/2 teaspoon vanilla

1 cup semi-sweet
  chocolate bits
1 cup chopped walnuts
3 to 4 tablespoons
  peppermint candy
  canes, crushed

Place egg whites in small bowl and beat with electric mixer at high speed until foamy. Add cream of tartar and salt and beat until soft peaks form. Add sugar one tablespoon at a time, beating after each addition. Meringue should be stiff and shiny. Fold in vanilla, chocolate bits, nuts, and candy. Drop by teaspoonfuls onto lightly greased cookie sheets, leaving about 1 1/2" space between cookies. Bake in a slow oven (250°F) for 40 minutes. Remove to wire racks to cool. Store in airtight container. MAKES ABOUT 5 DOZEN.

LAUREL GABEL

LIZZIES

1 pound golden raisins
1/2 cup bourbon
1/4 cup sweet butter
1/2 cup light brown sugar, firmly packed
2 eggs
1 1/2 cups flour
1 1/2 teaspoons baking soda

1 1/2 teaspoons cinnamon
1/2 teaspoon nutmeg
1/2 teaspoon ground cloves
1 pound pecan halves
1/2 pound citron, diced
1 pound candied cherries

Soak raisins in bourbon for at least 1 hour to plump. Cream butter and beat in sugar. Add eggs, beating well. Sift flour with baking soda and spices and add to butter mixture. Add drained raisins, nuts, and fruit. Drop by teaspoonfuls onto buttered cookie sheets. Bake at 325°F for about 15 minutes. Store in airtight containers. Cookies freeze well. MAKES 8 TO 10 DOZEN.

MONICA FORMAN *and* MARY BEVILACQUA *both submitted this recipe. Mary got it at the Lexington, Massachusetts, Holiday Fair in 1975.*

CANDY APPLE COOKIES

1/2 cup butter or marga-
  rine
1 teaspoon vanilla
1/2 cup confectioners'
  sugar

1/2 cup brown sugar,
  firmly packed
1 egg
2 cups flour

Coating:
36 light caramels
6 ounces evaporated milk
Few drops of red food
  coloring

Chopped nuts for rolling

Cream butter and vanilla until soft. Add confectioners' sugar and brown sugar and cream well. Add egg and beat until blended. Mix in flour and form dough into 1" balls. Bake on ungreased cookie sheets for 15 to 18 minutes at 350°F. Place a toothpick in each cookie while still warm.

To make coating: In top of double boiler over simmering water, melt caramels with evaporated milk and stir until smooth. Add red food coloring if desired. Dip cookies one at a time into caramel mixture, then roll in chopped nuts. Place in small paper muffin cups. MAKES ABOUT 30.

MARY BEVILACQUA: *"Another recipe from Gus Saunder's 'Yankee Kitchen' radio show. I made these one year for the Cookie Exchange."*

LEMON CHEESE COOKIES

1 cup butter, softened
6 ounces cream cheese
1/4 cup confectioners'
  sugar
2 1/4 cups flour

1 teaspoon grated lemon
  rind
1 teaspoon lemon juice
Confectioners' sugar

Filling:

1 pound (3 cups) cottage
  cheese
2 eggs
1 cup sugar

1/2 cup flour
1/4 cup lemon juice
1 tablespoon grated lemon
  rind

In a large bowl, combine butter, cream cheese, confectioners' sugar, flour, grated lemon rind, and lemon juice. Blend with a mixer until dough forms. Chill, covered, for 30 minutes.

Meanwhile, in a large saucepan, combine filling ingredients and blend well. Cook over medium heat, stirring constantly, until thick. Remove from heat. Divide chilled dough into 4 parts. Roll each part to a 9″ square, and cut into 3″ squares. Place 1 tablespoon of filling in the center of each square. Fold in half diagonally to make triangles, and press edges to seal. Place on greased cookie sheets, and bake at 350°F for 22 to 25 minutes. Sprinkle with confectioners' sugar when cool. MAKES 36 TRIANGLES.

LAUREL GABEL

CREAM CHEESE FOLDOVERS

1 pound pitted dates
1/2 cup water
1/2 cup sugar
1 cup butter, softened

8 ounces cream cheese
2 cups flour
1/2 teaspoon salt
Confectioners' sugar

Combine dates, water, and sugar in saucepan, and cook until thick, stirring constantly. Remove from heat. In bowl, cream butter until fluffy. Add cream cheese and beat well. Blend in flour and salt, mix well, and shape into two balls. Chill dough for several hours. Roll dough to 1/8" thick and cut into rounds with a 2" cookie cutter. Place 1 teaspoon date filling on each circle. Fold dough over, but don't pinch edges together. Place on greased cookie sheets and bake at 375°F for 15 minutes. Cool on rack, then sprinkle with confectioners' sugar. MAKES 3 DOZEN.

SUSAN MAHNKE PEERY: *"When we did an article about Kathy Donohue of Litchfield, Connecticut, in Yankee magazine's 'Great New England Cooks' series in 1982, we didn't have room to publish this recipe, although it was mentioned in the story. We were flooded with requests! This is only one of Kathy's excellent recipes."*

OLD-FASHIONED
MINCEMEAT-FILLED COOKIES

◆——◆

3 cups flour
1 teaspoon baking powder
1/2 teaspoon salt
3/4 cup butter, softened
1 1/2 cups sugar
2 eggs

1 tablespoon grated lemon
  rind
1 egg yolk
Sugar, for sprinkling

Filling:

1 cup prepared mincemeat
1/4 cup coarsely chopped
  walnuts

1 teaspoon lemon juice

Sift flour with baking powder and salt, and set aside. In large bowl, with electric mixer at medium speed, beat batter, 1 1/2 cups sugar, 2 eggs, and lemon rind until light and fluffy. With wooden spoon, beat in flour mixture until smooth. Form dough into a ball, wrap in plastic, and chill for several hours. Mix mincemeat, walnuts, and lemon juice. On a lightly floured board, roll out 1/4 of the dough at a time to 1/8″ thickness. With a 2 1/2″ scalloped or round cookie cutter, cut as many circles as possible, rerolling scraps. If desired, cut a center hole in half of the cookies. Place the solid cookies on greased cookie sheets and spread 1 teaspoon of filling over each cookie. Cover with reserved halves and seal firmly using a floured fork. Beat egg yolk with 1 teaspoon water and brush over tops of cookies. Sprinkle with granulated sugar. Bake at 375°F for 12 minutes, until nicely browned. Cool on rack.
MAKES ABOUT 40.

MARY BEVILACQUA

SANTA'S WHISKERS

1 cup butter
1 cup sugar
2 tablespoons milk
1 teaspoon rum flavoring
2 1/2 cups flour

3/4 cup red or green
  candied cherries,
  finely chopped
1/2 cup chopped pecans
3/4 cup shredded coconut

Cream butter and sugar. Blend in milk and rum flavoring. Stir in flour, cherries, and pecans. Form dough into two 8″ rolls. Roll dough in shredded coconut to coat. Wrap in waxed paper or plastic wrap and chill thoroughly, for several hours or overnight. Cut into 1/4″ slices. Place on ungreased cookie sheets and bake at 375°F for 12 minutes, until golden. MAKES ABOUT 60.

LEAH ROURKE: *"The cookies are rolled in coconut to resemble the jolly old man's beard!"*

POPPY SEED COOKIES

1/2 cup butter
2/3 cup sugar
1 egg
1 2/3 cups flour
1 1/2 teaspoons baking
  powder

Pinch of salt
Pinch of baking soda
1/2 teaspoon freshly
  grated nutmeg
2 tablespoons poppy seeds

Cream butter and sugar. Add egg and mix well. Add flour, baking powder, salt, baking soda, nutmeg, and poppy seeds and mix well. Batter will be stiff. Drop onto greased cookie sheets, flatten with a floured glass or custard cup, and bake at 350°F for about 15 minutes. MAKES ABOUT 30.

MARY BEVILACQUA: *"Miki Prencipe made these in 1983 for our Cookie Exchange."*

GLAZED PINEAPPLE DROP COOKIES

One 8-ounce can crushed
  pineapple, in natural
  juice
3 cups flour
1/2 teaspoon salt
1 teaspoon baking soda

1/2 cup butter, softened
1 1/2 cups sugar
2 eggs
1 teaspoon almond extract
1/2 cup chopped nuts, for
  sprinkling

Glaze:
1/4 cup soft butter
2 cups sifted confectioners'
  sugar

3 tablespoons pineapple
  juice

Drain pineapple, reserving juice for glaze. Sift together flour, salt, and baking soda and set aside. In a large bowl, cream butter and sugar until light and fluffy. Beat in eggs. Then beat in dry ingredients until just blended. Fold in crushed pineapple and almond extract. Drop by teaspoonfuls 2″ apart on greased cookie sheets. Bake at 350°F for 10 minutes. Cool. Make glaze by combining butter, confectioners' sugar, and pineapple juice. Spread glaze over cookies and sprinkle with chopped nuts. MAKES ABOUT 6 DOZEN.

LAUREL GABEL

10. THE COOKIE EXCHANGE BUFFET:
What to Serve While You're Waiting to Swop Cookies

CHRISTMAS PUNCH

1 quart cranberry juice
1 cup sugar
2 cups orange juice
1 cup pineapple juice
3/4 cup fresh or frozen
   lemon juice

1/2 teaspoon almond
   extract
2 cups chilled ginger ale
1 pint pineapple sherbet

Blend cranberry juice, sugar, fruit juices, and almond extract. Refrigerate, covered, until serving time. Just before serving, stir in ginger ale and sherbet. SERVES 10 TO 12.

MARY AND LAUREL

CIDER WASSAIL

4 cups fresh apple cider
1/4 to 1/3 cup dark brown
  sugar, firmly packed
1/2 cup dark rum
2 tablespoons brandy
2 tablespoons apple
  brandy (applejack)
1 tablespoon Grand
  Marnier
1/4 teaspoon cinnamon

1/4 teaspoon ground
  cloves
1/8 teaspoon ground
  allspice
Pinch of salt
1 rounded teaspoon orange
  juice concentrate
Whipped cream for
  garnish

Bring cider to boil. Add sugar and stir until dissolved. Remove from heat. Stir in rum, brandy, apple brandy, Grand Marnier, spices, and salt. Stir in orange juice concentrate. Place over moderate heat, stirring constantly, for about 2 minutes. Pour into demitasse cups or wineglasses and top with a generous amount of slightly sweetened whipped cream. Garnish with a grating of fresh nutmeg if desired. SERVES 10 TO 15.

> MARY AND LAUREL: *"The whipped cream makes a big difference in the finished taste of the drink—don't omit it."*

HOT CRANBERRY PUNCH

3/4 cup brown sugar,
  firmly packed
1/2 teaspoon nutmeg
1 teaspoon cinnamon
1/2 teaspoon allspice
1/2 teaspoon ground
  cloves
4 cups water

2 cans whole-berry
  cranberry sauce
1 quart unsweetened
  pineapple juice
1 tablespoon butter
1 cup diced fresh
  pineapple (optional)

Combine brown sugar with spices and add 1 cup of water. Bring to a boil in a large kettle. Add cranberry sauce, crushing with a wooden spoon. Add 3 cups water and stir until smooth. Pour in pineapple juice and simmer for 5 minutes. Just before serving, add 1 tablespoon butter. You may add diced fresh pineapple while the punch is simmering. The fruit absorbs the punch flavor and is a tasty bonus in the cup. SERVES 20.

PEG PEERY

PEACH BRANDY EGGNOG

6 egg yolks
1 cup confectioners' sugar
1 2/3 cups peach brandy
1 cup cold milk

1 pint heavy cream,
  whipped
Freshly grated nutmeg

In large bowl with electric mixer at medium speed, beat egg yolks until light. Gradually beat in sugar. Slowly pour in brandy while beating constantly. Let rest about 10 minutes. Gradually beat in milk. Refrigerate, covered, until well chilled (at least 3 hours). To serve, pour brandy mixture into chilled punch bowl. Gently fold in whipped cream just to blend. Grate nutmeg over top. MAKES 10 TO 12 SERVINGS.

MARY AND LAUREL

SANGRIA (RED OR WHITE)

2 gallons California
  Zinfandel or Chablis,
  chilled
2 quarts orange juice,
  chilled
2 cups lemon juice,
  chilled
1 cup sugar

1 cup brandy
1/2 cup Cointreau or
  Strega
2 quarts club soda, chilled
2 trays ice
3 thinly sliced oranges
3 thinly sliced lemons

Pour wine, juices, sugar, brandy, and liqueur into large
punch bowl and stir to blend. Add soda and ice. Float orange and lemon slices on top. MAKES ABOUT 3 GALLONS.

MARY AND LAUREL

DANISH PASTRY WREATH
WITH ALMOND FILLING

Dough:
1 1/2 cups butter
1/4 cup flour
3/4 cup milk
1/3 cup sugar
1 teaspoon salt

1/2 cup warm water
2 packages active dry
    yeast
1 egg
3 3/4 cups flour

Filling:
8-ounce can (1 cup)
    almond paste
3/4 cup (about 8) crushed
    Zwieback

1/2 cup butter, melted
1 egg
1/2 teaspoon almond
    extract

Frosting:
2 cups confectioners'
    sugar
3 to 4 tablespoons milk

Red and green candied
    cherries

In a bowl, beat butter and 1/4 cup flour with wooden spoon until smooth. Place a sheet of waxed paper on a wet surface to prevent slipping, and spread the butter-flour mixture on the paper in a 12" x 8" rectangle. Slip paper onto a cookie sheet and refrigerate. Heat milk slightly. Add sugar and salt and stir to dissolve. Cool to lukewarm. Pour the 1/2 cup warm water into a large bowl, sprinkle with yeast, and stir to dissolve. Stir in milk mixture, egg, and 3 cups flour. Beat with wooden spoon until smooth. Mix in remaining flour with hands until dough leaves sides of bowl. Refrigerate, covered, for half an hour. Turn out onto lightly floured pastry cloth, and using a stockinette cover on rolling pin, roll dough into a 16" x 12" rectangle. Place chilled butter mixture across half of dough; peel off paper. Fold other half of dough over butter and pinch edges to seal. With the fold at your right, roll out from the center to form a 16″ x 8″ rectangle. From the short side, fold dough into thirds, making three layers. Seal edges by pinching. Chill for 1 hour. Repeat this same rolling and folding step; seal edges again, and chill for 1/2 hour. (If butter breaks through, dust area with flour to prevent sticking.) Roll out a third time, fold as before, seal edges, and chill, wrapped in foil, for 3 hours or overnight.

Cut dough in half the long way, and roll one half into a 22″ x 8″ strip. (Chill the other half.) Cut the strip into thirds lengthwise. Combine the filling ingredients and mix well. Fill the center of each long strip with 1/3 cup of the filling mixture. Close the edges over the filling and pinch to seal. Braid loosely and form a wreath, leaving a 6″ inner opening, on brown paper on a cookie sheet. Seal ends together. Let rise in a warm place until doubled, about 1 hour.

Meanwhile, make another wreath using the second portion of dough. Preheat oven to 375°F. Bake each wreath, when ready, for about 1/2 hour, until golden. Cool partially on rack. Mix frosting and apply to slightly warm pastry. Decorate with candied red cherries, using green cherries cut into leaf shapes. MAKES 2 COFFEE RINGS.

> MARY AND LAUREL: *"Don't attempt this on a day when you have deadlines to meet. It is an all-day project requiring several rollings and foldings to achieve the buttery layers."*

DANISH PUFF

2 cups flour
1 cup butter
1 cup plus 2 tablespoons
water

1 teaspoon almond extract
3 eggs

Frosting:

1 1/2 cups confectioners'
sugar
2 tablespoons butter,
softened

1/2 teaspoon almond
extract
Boiling water
Sliced almonds, for sprinkling

Measure 1 cup of flour into bowl. Cut in 1/2 cup butter. Sprinkle with 2 tablespoons water and mix with a fork. Round into a ball and divide in half. Pat each half with hands into a long strip, 12" x 3". Place strips 3" apart on an ungreased cookie sheet. Mix remaining 1/2 cup butter with 1 cup water. Bring to a rolling boil. Add almond extract and remove from heat. Immediately add remaining 1 cup flour and stir briskly to keep it from lumping. When smooth and thick add one egg at a time, beating until smooth. Divide egg mixture in half and spread one half evenly over each strip of pastry. Bake at 350°F for about 1 hour, until topping is crisp and nicely browned. Frost when cool.

To make frosting: Combine confectioners' sugar, butter, almond extract, and enough boiling water to make a smooth icing. Spread over cooled almond puff and sprinkle generously with sliced almonds.

LUCILLE BILLINGS: *"When I bring this to the Cookie Exchange for Mary's dessert table, I decorate each loaf with red and green candied cherries."*

COUNTRY OPTIONS'
YULE LOG CAKE

◆━━━━━━━━━━━━━━━━━━━━━━━━━━━━━━━━━━━━━◆

Dough:
3 eggs
1 cup sugar
1/3 cup water
1 teaspoon vanilla

3/4 cup all-purpose flour
  or 1 cup cake flour
1 teaspoon baking powder
1/4 teaspoon salt

Filling:
1 cup whipping cream

3 tablespoons
  confectioners' sugar

Glaze:
1 cup heavy cream
10 ounces semi-sweet
  chocolate, chopped, or
  10 ounces chocolate
  chips

Meringue Mushrooms:
3 egg whites
1/4 teaspoon cream of tartar

3/4 cup sugar

Beat eggs on high speed until very thick and lemon-colored. (If eggs are not beaten enough, the cake will be heavy and rubbery.) Gradually beat in sugar. On low speed, beat in water and vanilla. Add dry ingredients gradually, beating just until batter is smooth. (To make chocolate-flavored batter, add 1/4 cup cocoa.)

Pour into a heavy jelly-roll pan that has been lined with greased and floured aluminum foil or waxed paper. Bake at 375°F for 12 to 15 minutes. Immediately loosen cake from edges of pan and invert onto a towel that has been sprinkled with flour (for plain cake) or cocoa (for chocolate cake). Remove foil or waxed paper. Trim edges of cake if necessary. While cake is still hot, carefully roll both cake and towel, starting with the narrow end, and place on wire rack to cool for at least 30 minutes.

To prepare filling: Whip cream until quite stiff, incorporating sugar as you whip. If desired, make cinnamon filling by adding 1/2 teaspoon cinnamon; cherry-almond filling by adding 1/4 cup chopped maraschino cherries, 1/4 cup chopped roasted almonds, and 1 teaspoon almond extract; mint filling by adding oil of peppermint to taste (and food coloring if desired).

Unroll cooled cake and remove towel. Spread filling over cake, being generous at edges. Roll up.

To prepare glaze: Combine cream and chocolate in heavy pot or in top of double boiler and heat until chocolate is completely melted and mixture is smooth, stirring constantly.

Spread chocolate glaze over roll. Run a fork's tines unevenly down the length of the cake to simulate bark. If desired, cut an angled slice from one end of the cake and affix to one side of the log (using glaze as "glue") to form a "knot." Use glaze to hold the slice and conceal the seam. Place meringue mushrooms at the joint. Use your imagination to decorate further.

To prepare meringue: Beat egg whites and cream of tartar until foamy. Beat in sugar 1 tablespoon at a time until mixture is stiff and glossy. Place meringue in pastry bag, and pipe "dots" of meringue for tops of mushrooms, and lines for stems. Sprinkle with cocoa for authentic-looking brown spots. Bake at 275°F until dried and lightly browned, about 1/2 hour. Join tops and stems with chocolate glaze. These meringues keep well if stored in an airtight container.

SANDY RAY: *"We have a small bed and breakfast inn, Country Options, in Ashland, New Hampshire, and we also run Divine Desserts Bakery. One of the holiday favorites is our Yule Log."*

ENGLISH TRIFLE

1 sponge cake
Cream sherry
Seedless raspberry
  preserves
4 egg yolks
5 to 6 tablespoons sugar
Pinch of salt
2 cups light cream
1 tablespoon cognac,
  white crème de cacao,
  or vanilla (more to
  taste)

1 cup heavy cream
Dash of cognac, vanilla, or
  sherry
Cherries
Nuts

Cut cake to fit in bottom of 12-cup capacity decorative bowl. Sprinkle liberally with cream sherry so that cake is damp, but not soggy. Allow cake to stand 15 minutes, then add more sherry if desired. Cover top and sides of cake with raspberry preserves. In mixing bowl, blend egg yolks, sugar, and salt. Heat light cream to boiling, stirring constantly. Gradually pour hot cream into egg mixture, stirring constantly. Cook over medium heat until custard coats spoon (3 or 4 minutes). Remove from heat. Add cognac, crème de cacao, or vanilla. Pour over cake. Let cool, then refrigerate, covered. Just before serving, whip 1 cup heavy cream flavored with a dash of cognac, vanilla, or sherry. Cover entire trifle. Garnish with cherries and nuts.
SERVES 8.

MARY AND LAUREL

MEXICAN PARTY CAKE

1 angel food cake
3/4 cup chocolate chips
1/2 teaspoon instant
  coffee
2 tablespoons water
4 eggs, separated

4 tablespoons sugar
1 teaspoon cinnamon
1/8 teaspoon ground
  cloves
1 cup heavy cream,
  whipped

Combine chocolate chips, coffee, and water in top of double boiler. Heat over hot water, stirring until chips melt and mixture is blended. Remove from heat and cool slightly. Beat in egg yolks one at a time. In a large bowl beat the egg whites until foamy, then add sugar and spices gradually. Beat until stiff. Fold the chocolate mixture into the egg whites, then fold in the whipped cream. Cut the cake horizontally into 3 layers. Fill the layers and cover the cake with the chocolate cream. Chill for at least 4 hours before serving. SERVES 12.

ROSALEE OAKLEY: *"I got this recipe more than twenty years ago while working in the Migrant Ministry in Clayton, New Jersey. My landlady, Mrs. Brown, served it one evening. Part of its popularity in our family lies in the fact that the frosting is not as sweet as most, yet is a perfect match for the cake."*

CASSATA ALLA SICILIANA

One 9" x 5" pound cake
1 pound ricotta cheese
1/4 cup sugar
3 tablespoons Grand
Marnier

1 10-ounce jar raspberry
jam
2 ounces semi-sweet
chocolate, coarsely
chopped

Frosting:
12 ounces (2 cups) semi-
sweet chocolate chips
3/4 cup cold, strong black
coffee

1 cup sweet butter, chilled
and cut into 1/2" pieces

Blend ricotta cheese and sugar until smooth. Cut pound cake horizontally into four slabs. Place the bottom slab on a serving plate and spread with one-quarter of the ricotta cheese. Freeze for 5 to 10 minutes, until ricotta is firm. Combine liqueur, jam, and chocolate, and spread one-quarter of this mixture over the ricotta. Freeze for 5 to 10 minutes. Repeat until all layers are assembled. Refrigerate for 2 hours.

To prepare frosting: Melt chocolate with cold coffee in a heavy saucepan over low heat. Stir constantly until smooth. Remove from heat and beat in butter, one piece at a time, until mixture is smooth. Refrigerate until mixture is of spreading consistency.

Frost cake, then cover loosely with plastic wrap and allow to "ripen" for 24 hours in the refrigerator before serving. Decorate as desired. MAKES 15 SERVINGS.

LAUREL GABEL

BEST CHEESECAKE

Crust:

1 1/2 cups graham cracker
  crumbs
3 tablespoons sugar

1/2 teaspoon cinnamon
1/4 cup unsalted butter,
  melted

Filling:

24 ounces cream cheese
1 1/4 cups sugar
6 eggs, separated
2 cups sour cream

1/3 cup flour
2 teaspoons vanilla
Grated rind of 1 lemon
Juice of 1/2 lemon

To make crust: Generously grease a 9" springform pan with butter. Place pan in center of a 12" square of aluminum foil and press foil up around side of pan. Combine graham cracker crumbs, sugar, cinnamon, and melted butter in a small bowl and blend well. Press crumb mixture onto bottom and sides of pan. Chill crust while making filling.

To make filling: Using electric mixer at low speed, beat cream cheese until soft. Gradually beat in sugar until light and fluffy. Beat in egg yolks one at a time. Stir in sour cream, flour, vanilla, lemon rind, and juice until smooth. Beat egg whites until they hold stiff peaks. Gently fold whites into cheese mixture until well blended. Pour into prepared pan. Bake at 350°F for 1 hour and 15 minutes. Turn the oven off (but keep the door shut) and allow cake to cool in oven for 1 hour. Remove to wire rack and cool to room temperature. Chill overnight before serving. SERVES 10 TO 12.

MARY AND LAUREL

CLAYTON CARROT CAKE

4 eggs
1 cup sugar
1 cup brown sugar, firmly
  packed
1 1/2 cups vegetable oil
2 cups flour
2 teaspoons baking
  powder
2 teaspoons baking soda

1/4 teaspoon salt
1 1/2 teaspoons cinnamon
1/2 teaspoon nutmeg
3 cups shredded carrots
1 cup raisins
1 teaspoon vanilla
1 cup walnuts or pecans,
  chopped

Beat eggs with sugars. Sift together dry ingredients. Add
dry ingredients and oil alternately to sugar mixture. Fold
in carrots, raisins, vanilla, and nuts. Pour into greased
bundt pan or 10″ tube pan. Bake at 375°F for 45 to 50
minutes. Cool cake in pan for 10 minutes, then turn out
on rack to cool completely. Frost when cool with Cream
Cheese Frosting. Spread generously over top and sides of
cake and sprinkle with finely chopped nuts. Garnish with
carrot curls if desired. SERVES 12 TO 15.

Cream Cheese Frosting:

8 ounces cream cheese
1/2 cup butter
2 teaspoons vanilla

1 pound confectioners'
  sugar
1/3 to 1/2 cup chopped
  nuts

Beat cream cheese with butter. Add vanilla and sugar. Beat
until light and fluffy.

MARY AND LAUREL

MISSISSIPPI
MUD PIE CAKE

5 squares unsweetened
  chocolate
1 3/4 cups strong coffee
1/4 cup bourbon
1 cup butter
2 cups sugar

2 eggs
2 cups flour
1 teaspoon baking soda
1/2 teaspoon salt
1 teaspoon vanilla
Cocoa

In top of double boiler over simmering water, heat chocolate, coffee, bourbon, and butter until chocolate is melted and smooth. Add sugar and mix well. Add eggs and mix well. Sift together flour, baking soda, and salt and add to chocolate mixture 1/2 cup at a time. Stir in vanilla. Butter a 9" tube pan and dust the surface with cocoa. Pour in the batter. Bake at 275°F for 1 hour and 30 minutes. Cool completely before cutting. SERVES 12 TO 15.

LAUREL GABEL

PINK AND PRETTY PARTY PIE

1 quart vanilla ice cream
2 cups fresh or frozen
   cranberries
1 cup sugar

1/2 cup chopped nuts
1 cup heavy cream,
   whipped

Soften ice cream slightly and press it into a 9″ pie pan to form a shell. Place in freezer and cover with plastic. Place cranberries in blender or food processor and chop well. Add sugar and blend well. Let stand overnight. Add chopped nuts and whipped cream to cranberries, folding cream in carefully. Spoon into frozen ice-cream shell. Refreeze for at least 4 hours. SERVES 6 TO 8.

JANET MEANY: *"This is a nice Christmas dessert—very pretty and easy."*

CRANBERRY DESSERT

2 cups finely chopped
  cranberries
1 large or 2 small bananas,
  sliced
2/3 cup sugar
2 cups crushed vanilla
  cookies

1/2 cup butter
1 cup confectioners' sugar
2 eggs
1/2 cup coarsely chopped
  nuts
1 cup heavy cream,
  whipped

Mix chopped cranberries, bananas, and sugar, and set aside. Put half of the crushed cookies in the bottom of an 8" x 8" pan. Cream butter and confectioners' sugar. Add eggs and beat well. Spread over the crumbs. Top with the cranberry-banana mixture. Sprinkle with nuts. Spread with whipped cream and remaining crumbs. Freeze for several hours before serving. SERVES 6 TO 8.

LAUREL GABEL

LEMON-ORANGE ANGEL DESSERT

1 tablespoon unflavored
  gelatin
4 tablespoons cold water
1 cup boiling water
3/4 cup sugar
Dash of salt
1 cup orange juice

1/2 cup lemon juice
Grated rind of 1 lemon
1 angel food cake
2 cups heavy cream
Chopped nuts
Shredded coconut

Soften gelatin in cold water. Add boiling water, sugar, and salt; stir. Add juices and rind and stir again. Refrigerate 2 to 3 hours, until slightly jelled and the consistency of un-beaten egg whites. Line a 2-quart bowl with waxed paper. Break angel food cake into small cubes and set aside. Whip one half of cream and fold into gelatin mixture. In lined bowl put layer of cream mixture and layer of cake cubes. Repeat, ending with cream mixture. Refrigerate 8 hours or overnight. Invert onto cake plate, peel off paper, and frost with remaining cream, whipped. Sprinkle with nuts and coconut if desired. SERVES 8.

MARY AND LAUREL

KIFLI

2 cups flour
1 cup butter
2 egg yolks, slightly
  beaten

1/2 cup sour cream

1 egg beaten with a little
water

Confectioners' sugar

Filling:
10 ounces walnuts,
  ground (about 2 cups)
1/2 cup sugar
1/4 cup light cream or
  milk

1 1/2 teaspoons almond
extract

Cut butter into flour with a pastry blender until the mixture resembles coarse crumbs. Add egg yolks and sour cream. Stir until just combined. Knead briefly on a lightly floured surface until dough is smooth. Shape into a flat round, wrap in plastic, and refrigerate.

To prepare filling: Combine nuts, sugar, milk, and extract. Blend well.

Preheat the oven to 400°F. On a lightly floured surface, roll out half of the dough until 1/8″ thick, roughly to a 12″ × 16″ rectangle. Cut into 4″ x 4″ squares. Paint the top of each square lightly with the egg and water wash (use a soft paintbrush or a pastry brush). Spread a rounded teaspoonful of filling diagonally down the center of each square. Bring opposite corners to center and overlap them, pinching to seal. Brush all over with egg wash and sprinkle lightly with sugar. Place about 2″ apart on greased cookie sheets. Bake for about 15 minutes, until nicely

browned. Cool on rack. Dust with confectioners' sugar.
MAKES ABOUT 2 DOZEN.

> LAUREL GABEL: *"This recipe can also make about 6 dozen small cookies. Cut the dough into two-inch squares instead of four-inch, and use less filling in each one. Proceed as in the original recipe."*

FRENCH FUDGE

3 cups (18 ounces) semi-sweet chocolate chips
One 15-ounce can sweetened condensed milk

1 1/2 teaspoons vanilla
1/2 cup nuts

Melt chocolate bits in a double boiler over simmering water. Stir until smooth, then add condensed milk and blend. Stir in vanilla and nuts. Spread in 8" x 8" pan lined with buttered waxed paper. Chill for several hours. Invert onto cutting surface, peel off paper, and cut into 48 squares.

MARY AND LAUREL

CHRISTMAS FUDGE

◆ ━━ ◆

2 cups sugar
3/4 cup evaporated milk
2 tablespoons butter
1/2 teaspoon salt

12 ounces (2 cups)
   chocolate chips
1 teaspoon vanilla
2 cups chopped pecans or
   walnuts

Bring sugar, milk, butter, and salt to a boil. Stir constantly. Boil for 2 minutes. Remove from heat and add chocolate chips. Stir until chips are melted, then add vanilla and nuts. Pour into a greased 8" x 8" pan and chill until firm.

> MAUREEN ZOCK: *"This recipe is best if butter is used: it adds to the creamy texture of the fudge, which truly melts in your mouth."*

PECAN PRALINES

◆ ━━ ◆

1 cup buttermilk
2 cups sugar
Pinch of salt
1 teaspoon baking soda

2 teaspoons vanilla
4 tablespoons butter
2 cups pecans

Combine buttermilk, sugar, salt, and soda in a deep kettle, and cook, stirring constantly, until mixture is mahogany brown in color. Remove from heat. Add vanilla and butter and beat until almost thick. Add nuts and drop by spoonfuls onto a cool surface to harden. MAKES ABOUT 3 DOZEN.

TERRY FLETTRICH ROHE

INDEX